Adrian Teal cut his caricaturiſt's teeth in the legenꟷʒ, ꟷpɪttɪng Image workſhop under the tutelage of Roger Law and Peter Fluck. As a profeſſional political cartooniſt he has put his acute eye to work for the *Sunday Telegraph,* the *Sun,* the *Daily Mail, Time Out, The Times Educational Supplement* and *The Scotſman,* amongſt others. His ſteady hand was more recently called upon to provide hiſtorical ſpreads for the *QI* Annuals and a regular cartoon ſlot for *Hiſtory Today.* This got him thinking about uſing his caricaturiſt's teeth, his acute eye, ſteady hand and perhaps ſome other underutiliſed bits to bring hiſtory to life whilſt his tabloid experiences naturally led him to the bawdieſt century on record. The reſult is the book you're now holding.

THE GIN-LANE GAZETTE

By Adrian Teal

Firſt publiſhed in 2012.
This edition publiſhed in 2014.

Unbound
4-7 Manchester Street, Marylebone, London, W1U 2AE
www.unbound.co.uk

Typeset by Liſa Hunter
Cover deſign by Mark Ecob

A CIP record for this book is available from the Britiſh Library

ISBN 978-1-78352-081-7 (pb)
ISBN 978-1-908717-75-7 (hb)

Printed and bound in India by Replika Press Pvt. Ltd

THIS VOLUME
IS MOST RESPECTFULLY INSCRIB'D

to thofe WORTHIES nam'd hereunder, who have deem'd the Author's
unworthy Labours as deferving of their invaluable *Guidance,*
Affiftance, & generous *Co-operation* :-

Mr. JOHN MITCHINSON, Mr. JUSTIN POLLARD, Mr. DAN KIERAN,
& Mr. XANDER CANSELL, *Boulevardiers,* & Gentlemen Publifhers of Diftinction ;
Mr. JOHN LLOYD C.B.E., *Imprefario* of Comedies for the Electrick
Theatre ; Mrs. LUCY INGLIS, Author & Hiftorian of *London & Weftminfter* ; Mifs
LISA HUNTER, the *Gazette's* matchlefs Typographer-In-Ordinary ; Mifs EMILY BRAND,
beneficent Hiftorian, Dinner Companion, & matchlefs Beauty ; Mifs VICTORIA BUCKLEY,
Blueftocking & Gadabout ; Mifs KIRSTY McLACHLAN, Agent & Counfellor ; Mifs
KATRINA GULLIVER *{No Relation},* Mufe & Courtefan *Manquée* ; Mrs. ANNE FINE,
Author of much-admir'd Novels ; Mifs RITA M. BOSWELL, Archivift of
Harrow School {& *diftant Relation of the efteem'd Author,* Mr. *JAMES BOSWELL}* ; Mifs
SHEENA SUKUMARAN, of *Langdale's Limited,* Purveyors of the fineft
Electuaries & Cordials ; Mifs KERRY PIPER, Hoftefs of note, & Battler 'gainft Infirmities ; Mifs
CAROL MADDOCK, of the *National Library of Ireland,* by the Courtefy of which eftimable
Inftitution the Intelligence from Mr. HENRY SANDFORD appears ; *The FROLICK,* peerlefs
Performers of beguiling *Baroque* Mufickal Entertainments from Georgian *London* ; curious
Readers feeking further Particulars are advif'd to confult the following electrick
Handbill : www.thefrolick.com ; Mrs. SUZANNE LOUAIL, of the *Greenwich Maritime*
Inftitute ; Mifs KAT BROWN, & Mrs. MELANIE CLEGG, Writers of *Web-logs* ; Mr.
MICHAEL RENDELL, Georgian Gentleman ; Mr. RICHARD BENNETT, Landlord of
the *Falkland Arms* Ale-houfe, Oxon., wherein might be found the *Throne of Human Felicity* ; Mifs
SIOBHAN HOFFMANN-HEAP, Lady of Tafte & Influence ; the Proprietors of
the Periodickal *HISTORY TODAY,* by whofe permiffion the DUC de CHARTRES
& Commodore CARACCIOLO appear ; Mr. RICHARD FITCH, Hiftorick Cook, &
Trencherman ; Mifs CAITLIN HARVEY, Author's Champion ; Mr. LARS THARP,
Authority on Antiquities, & Friend to Mr. HOGARTH ; Mifs KITTY PRIDDEN & Mifs
ROSE DEACON of *Bramfoy's,* Purveyors of living Hiftory ; Mr. GEORGE HORNBY, mine
Hoft at the very excellent *Black's Club, Soho* ; Mrs. HELEN CHESSHIRE, Champion of Gin,
Worker of Miracles ; M'Lady HALLIE RUBENHOLD, Chronickler of Scandal, Smut, &
Whoremongery ; Dr. JENNI BARCLAY, Authority upon all matters volcanick ; Mifs KAREN
PAGE, Diffeminator of Hand-bills ; Mr. & Mrs. GRAHAM TEAL, patient Progenitors ; &
fundry Patrons of *Twitter's* famous Prattle Engine — too numerous to name — without whofe kindnefs
this poor Affemblage could never have entertain'd any Hope of enjoying the light of Day.

I am
Your moft obedient, oblig'd,
& very humble Servant,

Mr. ADRIAN TEAL Efq.,
Amanuenfis to Mr. NATHANIEL CROWQUILL.

FRONTISPIECE

Mr. NATHANIEL CROWQUILL Eſq.

Founder, Proprietor, & Editor of

The GIN-LANE GAZETTE

The

GIN-LANE GAZETTE

Being an Engrav'd

COMPENDIUM of ARTICLES

from that Periodickal,

during the Years 1750–1800,

Selected for the Satisfaction of Divers READERS & PATRONS

by its Founder & Editor

Mr. NATHANIEL CROWQUILL Efq.

Quidquid agunt homines, votum timor ira voluptas
Gaudia difcurfus noftri farrago libelli eft. JUVENAL

LONDON:

Printed for the Proprietor & Sold by **A. CULLY**, at the *Strutting Cock* in *St Paul's Churchyard*,
where Advertifements, & Letters to the Authors, are taken in.

MDCCCI

An INTRODUCTION To The WORK

WHEREAS YOUR WORSHIPS *see fit to honour this trifling* Opus *with Your Patronage,* I *beg leave to make an Introduction.* My *name is* NATHANIEL CROWQUILL, *& for these Fifty Years past I have been the humble Founder, Owner & Editor of the News-paper known to my loyal Readership as* The GIN-LANE GAZETTE.

My eyefight & Bladder not being what they once were, I have refolv'd to efcape the Fury & Cloacal Stench of *London,* to fettle in quiet retirement with my widow'd Sifter in *Northamptonshire,* tho' not before undertaking a moft PLEASANT TASK which a great many of my gracious Readers have been fo kind as to afk of me.

In half a Century, Fortune has fupply'd my beloved *Gazette* with more remarkable Narratives than I can number. In the light of announcing an intention to relinquifh my pofition in Publick Life, requefts for me to bring forth a *Volume* of my Periodickal's moft *Celebrated* Artickles have become too loud & too numerous to difmifs.

As a confequence, what you will here find refpectfully lay'd before You is a *COMPENDIUM* of fome of the Mifhaps, Scandals, Crimes, Accomplifhments & Failures which have befallen, fham'd, bedevill'd, elevated & afflicted both the great & the infamous Men & Women of our Age. And *what* an Age ! What a time to walk the *Earth* ! What wondrous lives have been led ; what remarkable Difcoveries made ; what tantalifing Goffip fpoken of ; what Talent, Trumpery, Celebrity, Villainy, Invention, Bravery & Folly have fhaken our World ! O *tempora* ! O *mores* !

But I run ahead of myfelf ! 'Tis not for a lowly chronickler of Events to try to influence your Opinion of thefe extraordinary & *hiftorick* Years. I fhall leave it to Your Worfhips to pafs judgment upon our Times, as defcrib'd & fet down in the enfuing pages. And I wifh you great joy of it.

I have the Honour to remain
Your Worfhips' Moft Humble & Oblig'd Servant,

Nathaniel Crowquill Efq.
January 16, 1801.

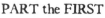

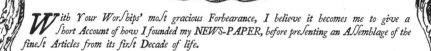

CROWQUILL

With Your Worships' most gracious Forbearance, I believe it becomes me to give a short Account of how I founded my NEWS-PAPER, before presenting an Assemblage of the finest Articles from its first Decade of life.

There being naval connexions on my Mother's side of our Family, it was decided that the opportunities of Preferment afforded by the maritime life would spur on a young man of Ability & Ambition. In 1748, as a stripling of Eighteen Years, & with a Warrant from *Surgeon's Hall* & letters of introduction, I hence found myself Surgeon's Mate in the Navy of His Britannic Majesty King GEORGE II, serving aboard the Frigate *Coxcomb*. My Superior was *Dr. SHINSAW*, a kindly man who taught me much concerning the Horrors of *Injury & Disease* aboard the King's Ships. I confess I soon came to know something of these Horrors at First hand when, after a Year's Sailing on the Indian Ocean, I was attack'd by a Sea-Bird, while engag'd at the Heads. The wound – to the privy parts of my Anatomy – putrefy'd alarmingly, & after a Month's convalescence in a stifling hot Cabin, I decided life upon the High Seas no longer gave me Pleasure. I return'd to my home, & some familial Disapprobation, in the County of Northamptonshire.

SHINSAW

In *February* of 1749, my dear Father died of an Inflammatory Distemper, & bequeath'd to me a small Legacy. Since I had enjoy'd keeping a Journal of my Life at sea, I form'd a Design of venturing forth for LONDON, there to try my luck as a Man of Letters in the world of News-papers. This I did with little delay, & after contributing Prose to many Publications for meagre remuneration, I decided upon a course of Action. If I was ever to make my Fortune, it was an indispensable necessity that I should write, print & sell my own Periodickal. In the interests of Oeconomy, I took rooms above the premises of *Mr. GRIPE*, a Pawnbroker in Gin-Lane, in the parish of *St. Giles-in-the-Fields* – a singularly noisome neighbourhood of Rookeries – & began upon the Adventure of my new Enterprise.

GRIPE

To enliven the pages of my News-sheet, I engag'd the services of *Mr. ISAAC JAKES*, an Artist & Engraver of great Ability, tho' apt to spend more time in the Spunging House, & in gratifying his base Appetites in our local taverns, than ever he did at his etchings. I shall not mislead you, Dear Readers : those early days were exceeding hard. Profit & Fame seem'd a distant Dream. Yet I persever'd, & Success cannot elude the grasp indefinitely of a man of Purpose. With the crapulent but talented Mr. Jakes in my employ, & with Determination urging me onward, I felt certain that *The GIN-LANE GAZETTE* would soon become requir'd reading for the *Beau Monde* in that Capital of the World, London.

My first Edition came off the Press in *April* of 1750, even as a most fearsome Series of EARTHQUAKES was spreading PANICK through our great City.

The Gin-Lane Gazette

PUBLISHED in LONDON — *April, 1750.* — Nathaniel Crowquill Efq.

The *Late* EARTHQUAKES & *The* FLIGHT *of* LONDON's CITIZENRY.

By Nathaniel Crowquill, Editor.

At around Midday on the 8th of February laſt, there was felt a ſlight E A R T H Q U A K E in *London*, & tho' it diſcomfited the Populace, it ſignify'd little. At half-paſt Five in the Morning, precifely one Month later – the 8th of March – a Second Quake of greater Magnitude ſhook the City, ſtarting many from their Slumbers, flinging down two old houſes, toppling ſtones from the Spire of *Weſtminſter Abbey*, & chiming the bells in many Steeples. Dogs howl'd in uncommon tone, & the fiſh in the Thames were ſeen to jump half a Yard above the water. We are given to underſtand a ſervant maid was thrown from her bed in *Charterhouſe-Square*, & ſuffer'd a broken Arm.

In anticipation of a Third Earthquake & yet greater Calamities on the impending 8th of April, *London's* Citizens, jaundic'd with Fear, began to flee the City in droves, & ſlept in the open air upon the Slopes of *Hampſtead, Highgate*, & *Iſlington*. The threats of diſreputable News-sheets to publiſh Liſts of All the *Nobility* & *Gentry*, who were to leave this place through *Fear of another Earthquake*, had no diſcernible Effect upon the numbers of fugitives. On the evening of the 5th of April, the roads out of London were crowded with carriages, & many ſat in their coaches all Night in *Hyde Park*, paſſing their Time at cards by the light of Candles.

Perhaps more diſquieting than any Earthquake has been the ſudden Proliferation of *Charlatans* & *Mountebanks* ſeeking to profit by theſe Events. The Mantua-makers have ſold great Numbers of *Earthquake Gowns* to fearful Ladies ſleeping out of doors, & a country Quack has been peddling Pills which he vows are *good againſt an Earthquake*. A Shoemaker of *Carnaby Market* claim'd to have been viſited by an Angel foretelling the certain Deſtruction of the World on the 8th of April, & a mad Lifeguardſman was arreſted & carry'd to Bedlam for ſtirring Panick with his fearful Prophecies.

The BISHOP of *LONDON* averr'd that the Earthquakes were a Judgment from GOD upon the City, to puniſh the trade in bawdy Prints & Books, citing Mr. JOHN CLELAND's infamous Novel, *The MEMOIRS of a WOMAN of PLEASURE*, as the principal ſpur to the Almighty's Wrath. He condemn'd the Book – chronickling the amatory Adventures of its abandon'd heroine, *Fanny Hill – as an open Inſult upon Religion & Good Manners, & a Reproach to the Honour of the Government, & the Law of the Country.* Mr. CHARLES WESLEY preach'd a ſermon alſo, & bade us *prepare to meet our GOD.*

We are happy to record that the 8th of April came, & paſſ'd, without Incident.

Price : Twopence Halfpenny.

The GAOL FEVER at The OLD BAILEY.

We are now able to furnifh our Readers with an Account of the terrible breaking out of the GAOL FEVER which afflicted many Perfonages at the *Old Bailey* Courts between the 17th & the 19th Days of laft Month.

It is thought that the Contagion was carry'd into the Court by prifoners brought to Trial at the City *Quarter Seffions*, & SIXTY SOULS are now fear'd to have perifh'd. It would appear that the deceaf'd were all feated on the Court's left-hand fide. Moft eminent amongft thefe Unfortunates are Sir SAMUEL PENNANT, the LORD MAYOR ; Three Juftices,

one of whom we name as Mr. JUSTICE ABNEY ; an Alderman, Sir DANIEL LAMBERT ; an Under-Sheriff ; & Eight members of the *Middlefex* Jury.

Poefies of flowers are now carry'd by Court-goers as Preventatives againft this virulent Diftemper, & henceforth fweet-fmelling Herbs fhall be fpread about the Benches in the hope of keeping the Contagion in abatement.

The MEMOIRS of HANNAH SNELL, The FEMALE SOLDIER.

This Month is publifh'd by Mr. ROBERT WALKER a moft diverting & fingular Work, entitl'd The FEMALE SOLDIER : or *The Surprifing Life & Adventures of HANNAH SNELL.* The particulars of Hannah's remarkable Life are broadly thefe :-

Hannah was born at Worcefter in 1723, & at the Age of Seventeen Years, departed that City to live with her marry'd Sifter in *Wapping.* Three Years hence, a *Fleet* Parfon coupl'd her to a Dutch Sailor call'd JAMES SUMMS, who abandon'd her foon thereafter, even tho' his bride was great with Child. The Infant liv'd but Five Months, & upon its demife, Hannah array'd herfelf in male Cloaths, & fet out in Purfuit of her faithlefs *Beau.*

company's Sergeant, who had her ftript to the Waift & flogg'd, yet fhe was able to conceal her true Sex by throwing herfelf quickly againft the Gate of *Carlifle Caftle,* thus hiding her Breafts from the affembl'd Soldiery. This *ill* ufage led her to defert when her Regiment was at *Portfmouth.* Wafting little time, fhe enlifted in the *Marines,* going aboard the Sloop *Swallow,* of ADMIRAL BOSCAWEN's Fleet. During this period of Service, fhe once again receiv'd a flogging, but upon this Occafion hid her woman's Phyfiognomy by means of a Scarf. At *Madras,* fhe faw Action againft the French at *Pondicherry,* where fhe had the misfortune to receive wounds in her Legs, but efcap'd the fcene of Battle, & was affifted in her Convalefcence at *Cuddalore* by an Indian woman.

Her fearching lafted near Five Years, during which time fhe enlifted under the Name of JAMES GRAY in a Regiment of Foot, raif'd to confront the Jacobite Menace of 1745. She made an Enemy of the

She return'd to England aboard HMS *Eltham,* whereupon fhe confefs'd her true Sex, & was difcharg'd. She has been allow'd a Penfion of 5d *per diem* by the Royal Hofpital, & it is rumour'd that *His Grace The DUKE of CUMBERLAND* has granted her an additional Annuity of £18.5s. She may fhortly be feen, by curious Readers, difporting herfelf in full regimental Drefs on the Stage of *The Royalty Theatre in Stepney, at Sadler's Wells, & at Goodman's Fields Theatre, Whitechapel.*

Of The APPREHENSION of Mr. MACLEAN, the *Gentleman* HIGHWAYMAN.

The Conversation of the Town being so much turn'd upon the *Gentleman Highwayman*, some Account of his Capture will be expected. On the 27th of this Month, Mr. JAMES MACLEAN was seiz'd & carry'd before *Justice* LEDIARD.

He was charg'd with robbing Mr. JOSIAH HIGDEN in the *Salisbury* Coach, near *Turnham Green*, on the previous Day. We understand that later that same Evening, he robb'd the *EARL of EGLINTON* of valuables, Cloaths, & a Blunderbuss, in his Carriage on *Hounslow Heath*. A Pawnbroker identify'd some of the Items as stolen, & as a consequence Maclean was unmask'd as a felon. His bold Accomplice, one WILLIAM PLUNKETT – a former Apothecary who acted the part of his Servant – has thus far eluded Capture. Perhaps the most infamous of all Mr. Maclean's Exploits was his assault last Year upon the *Hon.* H O R A C E WALPOLE, in *Hyde Park*. Maclean's Pistol, discharging accidentally,

graz'd the skin under Mr. Walpole's eye, leaving marks of shot upon his Face. Had he sat but an Inch to his Left, the ball must surely have enter'd his Head. Maclean had deliver'd to Mr. Walpole the next Morning a most courteous Letter, in which he assur'd that Gentleman that no Harm had been intended toward him, & that his Valuables might be restor'd for the Sum of 40 Guineas.

MACLEAN had handsome Lodgings in *St. James's-street*, & had been passing himself off as an Irish gentleman of £700 *per annum*. Indeed, so perfectly did he maintain this Deception that he was nearly marry'd to a young Lady of Fortune in *Chelsea*.

We hear the Highwayman has made a full Confession of the INFAMOUS CRIMES with which he has been charg'd.

The UNASSUAGEABLE GLUTTONY of Mr. HANDEL Reveal'd.

An unseemly Quarrel has lately broke out betwixt Mr. JOSEPH GOUPY, the Engraver of Mayfair, & the peerless Composer, Mr. GEORGE FRIDERIC HANDEL. Mr. Handel offer'd Mr. Goupy Hospitality at his House in Brook-Street, yet stated in most regretful terms that only plain Victuals were to be had. Mr. Goupy was pleas'd to accept the Invitation, & begg'd his Host most cordially not to concern himself over such a trifling Consideration.

Yet, when the Two Friends were some way into their meagre Repast, Mr. Handel excus'd himself, & left the Room for a considerable time. Curious as to his Companion's whereabouts, Mr.

Goupy made his way to the Parlour, & there, through a chink in the Door, spy'd Mr. Handel stuffing his Face with such Delicacies as he had lamented his Inability to afford his Friend.

We fear Mr Handel's unexampl'd Discourtesy has set such an affront to Mr. Goupy's Honour, that their eternal Estrangement is now assur'd, & we understand that the Engraver intends to publish a satirickal print of Mr. Handel in which he shall be portray'd as an engorg'd PIG, or *Harmonious Boar*, performing at his Organ, & surrounded by extravagant Comestibles, the like of which he denies his Friends.

Of the late Mr. EDWARD BRIGHT, the FATTEST MAN that ever liv'd in *ENGLAND*.

There died on the 10th Day of *November*, at the Age of Twenty-nine Years, one EDWARD BRIGHT, who was celebrated in the Town of *Maldon* & elsewhere as the largest man that this Kingdom has ever known.

As a Child, Mr. Bright was employ'd as a Post-boy, riding each Day from *Maldon to Chelmsford*, but was forc'd to abandon this position at the age of Twelve Years due to his weight, which was 12 Stones. In latter Years, he traded as a Grocer & Candle-merchant, & liv'd in a House in the High-street, next to the Church. By the Age of Twenty-eight, he weigh'd near 42 Stones, his Cheft measuring 5 Feet & 6 Inches, & his Belly measuring Six Feet & 11 Inches. It is said that his

Corpulence *so overpower'd his Strength that his Life was a Burden, & his Death a Deliverance.* He is mourn'd greatly, for he was allow'd by all a valuable & affable Friend, & a tender Father.

A Coffin of prodigious Dimensions was constructed to accommodate his Bulk, & the Staircase & part of a Wall of his House were taken away to allow the Corpse's removal. He was pull'd to the Church of *All Saints* upon a carriage, slid upon Rollers to the Vault, & bury'd with the use of a Triangle & Pulley.

A Wager was lately made in a *Maldon* Ale-house that *Seven-hundred Men* might fit inside the late Mr. Bright's capacious Waistcoat. This was achiev'd by underhand means, since Seven Men of the *Essex* Hundred of *Dengie* perform'd the Feat comfortably.

To make CHICKEN in a BOTTLE.

Take a Chicken, & take out all the Bones, being sure to keep the Head aside, & observing not to cut too much Skin from the Neck of the Bird. You must have a Bottle of thin Glass, with a wide Neck, & put in the Chicken as straight as you can, taking care to have the Opening of the Bird's Neck at the Top of the Bottle. Fill it almost Half-full with a *Farce*. This *Farce* should be made with Veal, Beef-marrow, Bacon, the Crumbs of a *French* Roll soak'd in Cream, & the Yolks & whipp'd Whites of 2 Eggs, all season'd with Salt, Pepper, & Nutmeg.

You must also have ready a little *Ragout*, made of thin Slices of Chicken, Partridge, Truffles, Cocks-combs wetted with Broth, & season'd. It should be thicken'd with *Cullis à la Reine*, made with stew'd Veal, Ham, Carrots, Sweet Herbs, Lemon, Garlick, Cloves, & Flour, strain'd off.

Put the *Ragout* into your Chicken, & thereafter fill the Bird with the rest of your *Farce*. Tie the Head of the Chicken over the Neck of the Bottle. You must boil the Bottle with its Bird for Three Hours in Water, & take care none goes inside. When you are ready to serve, cut the Bottle with a Diamond, that those who are seated at the Table may take the Chicken out for themselves.

Coq au Gin

The Gin-Lane Gazette

PUBLISHED in LONDON   *March, 1751.*   Nathaniel Crowquill Efq.

Of The PRINCE of WALES, KILL'D By A CRICKET BALL, & The Great Hardſhips This Will Occaſion the Silk-Weavers.

By Nathaniel Crowquill, Editor.

It is with the greateſt Sadneſs that we muſt inform our Readers of the untimely Demiſe of *His Royal Highneſs*, The PRINCE of WALES. Prince FREDERICK fell ill while dancing at *Leiceſter Houſe* on the Twentieth Day of this Month, and died ſuddenly. His Death has been attributed to an Injury he ſuſtain'd Two Years ago.

It was while playing a Game of *CRICKET* at *Cliveden, in Buckinghamſhire*, that His Highneſs was ſtruck hard in his Side by a Ball. An ABCESS form'd upon his Lung, would not heal theſe Two Years, & is confider'd the Cauſe of Death by *Phyſicians Royal*.

The deceas'd ſhall be bury'd at *Weſtminſter Abbey*. We alſo underſtand that a Memorial Game of *Cricket* in His Late Majeſty's Honour is plann'd to take place this July, at *Saltford Meadow*, in *Bath*.

The Prince's royal Parents have aſſerted that their Son was *the greateſt ASS, the greateſt Villain, the greateſt Liar, & the greateſt BEAST in all the World*, but have elected to adhere to Propriety, commanding that there ſhall be a Six-Month Period of Mourning. All Publick Entertainments ſhall ceaſe, & the Quality ſhall wear deep Black Cloaths & muffl'd Shoes for Three Months. Thereafter, Mourners are permitted to wear Grey, if they ſo wiſh. Yet, while many welcome theſe Obſervances as fit & becoming, the *SILK-WEAVERS* of *Spital-Fields*, who compriſe ſome 15,000 Souls, are afear'd that the Effects upon their Trade in gaudy Fabricks ſhall be calamitous beyond all poſſible deſcription.

Others are making light of the Prince's Paſſing, & a popular Verſe about His Highneſs is being circulated :-

Here lies poor FRED, who was alive & is dead,
Had it been his Father I had much rather,
Had it been his Siſter nobody would have miſs'd Her,
Had it been his Brother, ſtill better than another,
Had it been the whole Generation, ſo much better for the Nation,
But ſince it is FRED who was alive & is dead,
There is no more to be ſaid!

Price : Twopence Halfpenny.

THE EDITOR was highly gratify'd to receive a moſt frolickſome Verſe, from an ANONYMOUS Correſpondent taking the part of a lyrickal GIN HAG, & we publiſh it here, unexpurgated, for the Benefit of our Readers :-

STRIP ME NAKED, or ROYAL GIN FOR EVER.

I MUST, I will have GIN ! – that Skillet take,
Pawn it. – No more I'll roaſt, or boil or bake.
This Juice immortal will each want ſupply ;
Starve on, ye brats ! So I bung my Eye.
Starve ? No ! This GIN ev'n Mother's milk excels,
Paints the pale cheeks, and Hunger's darts repels.
The Skillet's pawned already ? Take this Cap ;
Round my bare Head I'll yon brown paper wrap.
Ha ! Half my Petticoat was torn away
By dogs (I fancy) as I maudlin lay.
How the Wind whiſtles through each broken Pane !
Through the wide-yawning roof how pours the Rain !
My Bedſtead's cracked ; the table goes hip-hop. –

But ſee ! The GIN ! Come, come, thou cordial drop !
Thou ſovereign Balſam to my longing Heart !
Thou Huſband, Children, all ! We muſt not part !
ſDrinksſ Delicious ! O ! Down the red Lane it goes ;
Now I'm a Queen, and trample on my Woes.
Inſpired by GIN, I'm ready for the road ;
Could ſhoot my Man, or fire the King's abode.
Ha ! My Brain's cracked. – The room turns round
                                          and round ;
Down drop the platters, pans : I'm on the Ground.
My tattered Gown ſlips from me. – What care I ?
I was born naked, and I'll naked die.

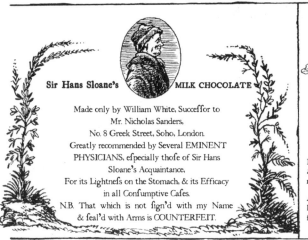

PARLIAMENT Sanctions GIBBETING.

Scarcely creditable tho' it may be to our Readers that such a Meafure has been fo long delay'd, the GIBBETING of certain Species of *Malefactor* in this Realm is only now fanction'd by the MURDER ACT, which laft Month *Parliament* faw fit to pafs.

The ACT makes plain Stipulation that this Practice fhould be referv'd for the moft heinous of Villains, amongft whom are Highwaymen, Sheep-ftealers, Robbers of the *Royal Mail,* & Murderers. Any mifcreant the Crown deems deferving of Capital Punifhment is to be hang'd within the compafs of Forty-eight Hours of their Conviction, *Sundays* excepted, & only the cadavers of murderers are to be given up to the Anatomifts for publick Diffection.

Of The ADOPTION of The GREGORIAN KALENDAR.

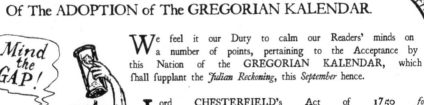

Mind the GAP!

We feel it our Duty to calm our Readers' minds on a number of points, pertaining to the Acceptance by this Nation of the GREGORIAN KALENDAR, which fhall fupplant the *Julian Reckoning,* this *September* hence.

Lord CHESTERFIELD's Act of 1750 *for Regulating the Commencement of the Year* having been ratify'd, the Second day of *September* fhall be follow'd by the 14th Day of *September,* & the new Year fhall henceforth begin on the 1ft Day of *January,* not *Lady Day,* the 25th Day of *March.* The *Exchequer,* being a law unto itfelf, has refuf'd to comply with the Adjuftment, & fhall adhere to the Obfervance of the *quondam* Syftem, refulting in the termination of the Taxation Year Eleven Days after the 25th Day of *March,* being the 5th Day of *April.*

The *Britifh* People fhall fuffer NO REAL TEMPORAL LOSS, or SHORTENING of LIFE, either by the excifion of thefe Eleven Days from their *Kalendar,* or owing to the Year 1751 having been of only Two-hundred & Eighty-two Days' duration. Left certain *Anti-Popifh* Objections be raif'd, in certain quarters, to a Syftem carrying the name of the late Pontiff, *Gregory,* the Act nowhere employs the word *Gregorian,* & the new Plan is known only as the *Britifh Kalendar.*

Mr. HENRY BLACKER, *The British* GIANT : An *Entertainment.*

Your EDITOR efteems it an Honour to render Felicity & Satisfaction to his Readers in acquainting them with new Entertainments which fhall excite their Curiofity.

Mr. HENRY BLACKER, of *Cuckfield* in the *County* of *Effex*, alfo known as *The Wonderful Giant*, & *The Modern Coloffus*, may be feen at *Half-Moon Court*, adjoining *Ludgate*, in a commodious Room, by any Number of Perfons, from Nine in the Morning till Nine at Night.

Mr. Blacker is pronounc'd by all a *Phenomenon of Nature*, ftanding Seven Feet & Four Inches tall, & he has had the Honour of being infpected by *His Grace* The DUKE of CUMBERLAND, by a great Number of the *Nobility*, by venerable Members of the *Royal Society*, & by Ladies & Gentlemen who delight in natural Curiofities, all of whom allow that he is of prodigious Height, & the beft proportion'd of his Size that ever was feen.

The EARL of MARCH has won a Wager by the moft vulpine of means, & in fo doing has greatly increaf'd his Fame in the matter of Shrewdnefs. He declar'd that he could convey a Letter a Diftance of Fifty Miles in One Hour only. This affertion being taken as foolifh *Gafconade*, & the ftake being put up, the Earl fet about proving his Claim.

He engag'd Twenty Cricketers of his acquaintance, renown'd for their Skill in catching & throwing, & bade them ftand in a meafur'd Circle. Having calculated the neceffary Number of throws each would have to make in this Circuit to cover the Diftance agreed, his Lordfhip plac'd the Letter in a Cricket Ball, which the Gentlemen toff'd to one another with fuch fpeed & dexterity that it was found the Letter had travell'd many Miles farther than the allotted Span.

The Gin-Lane Gazette

PUBLISHED in LONDON   *April, 1754.*   Nathaniel Crowquill Efq.

The CLAMOUR for *Fleet* WEDDINGS as a Confequence of the MARRIAGE ACT.

*L*ord *HARDWICKE's* MARRIAGE ACT of laft Year having come into Effect on the 25th Day of March, there broke out an indecorous Clamour on the part of many of our Citizenry to be wed betimes, & there is vociferous Oppofition to the Bill by thofe who confider it an Infringement of Liberty, which is held dear by every true *Englifhman.*

*T*he Act feeks to bring to an end thofe clandeftine Marriages & their concomitant Difficulties, which have thriv'd under the previous Syftem, whereby a Man & a Woman might be coupl'd in Matrimony by the fimple Expedient of exchanging Vows before Witneffes. It is doubtlefs the cafe that many a marriageable Heirefs has been dup'd by a falfe-hearted Debtor ; that Parifh Officers have made the baftard Progeny of Paupers the trouble of other Parifhes by marrying their Beggars beyond their bounds ; that many Innocents, too young to wed without the Confent of Parents, have been join'd irrevocably ; & that countlefs drunken Sailors & their Sweethearts have ftagger'd before a Parfon to plight their Troths, only to wake rueful & penitent upon the next Forenoon. The purlieus of the *Fleet Prifon* are moft infamous as the Refuge of bafe & avaricious Clergymen, who will make a Union for no greater reward than a Quartern of Gin.

What GOD hath join'd together let no Man put afunder!

*T*hefe Concerns not withftanding, the 24th Day of March (being the Day before the Act was enforc'd) faw Forty-five couples join'd in *Fleet* Ceremonies by 11 of the Clock that Morning, & near an Hundred Pair in Wedlock before the Day was out.

*T*he Act fhall undoubtedly terminate the Career of the excommunicant Minifter, Mr. ALEXANDER KEITH, who conducted innumerable clandeftine Weddings in *Hanover Square,* moft notorious amongft which were thofe of *Lord GEORGE BENTINCK, The* 6th *DUKE of HAMILTON, VISCOUNT STRANGE,* & *The DUKE of CHANDOS.* Within the Compafs of a Twelvemonth, Mr. Keith marry'd 723 Couples for his cuftomary 1-Guinea Fee, & for his pains was cut off from the Church on Epifcopal orders, after which Mr. Keith brazenly made to Excommunicate the very Bifhop he had fo anger'd. He was committed to the *Fleet Prifon* as a Confequence, yet continu'd in his Trade, importuning Four *Fleet* Parfons to conduct Weddings on his behalf, & putting his Name to the Marriage Certificates. He went fo far as to advertife his Services in the News-fheets, & we are told he has join'd around 6,000 Couples. He was forbidden to attend the Funeral of his Wife, fo had her embalm'd & difplay'd in a Shop in *South Audley Street,* ftating that fhe would not be bury'd until his Releafe. On the 24th Day of March aforefaid, Mr. Keith prefided over his final Sixty-one Marriages.

N.C., *Editor.*

Of *Capt.* HERVEY, ABDUCTED by an AMOROUS WIDOW.

You have Permission to come aboard, Sir!

One of our moſt able Sons of Neptune, *Captain AUGUSTUS HERVEY*, is perhaps as infamous as any of the ſeafaring Tribe for enjoying the Embraces of an infatuating jade in every Port, yet even he muſt have conſider'd himſelf bleſſ'd with greater *Fortune* than ever fell to the lot of one Man when his SKILL *as a* LOVER was harneſſ'd in a highly inventive manner.

Capt. Hervey lately weigh'd Anchor in Portugal, during which Sojourn he was abducted at the point of a Firearm, & carry'd through the Night, all the while in fear of his Life, to a myſterious Houſe. There was he uſher'd into the Bed-chamber of an arch & handſome Lady, whoſe Charms ſoon conquer'd his Trepidation, & arouſ'd his Paſſions. He enter'd plum into the ſpirit of the Hour, & the Pair embark'd upon a nocturnal Voyage of *Venery*.

The Lady ſwore our *Hero* to Secrecy, & he was pleaſ'd to rehearſe their amatory Adventure at her beheſt on a number of further Occaſions. Capt. Hervey has now identify'd his Seductreſs as HENRIETTE-JULIE-GABRIÈLE de LORRAINE, *The DUCHESS of CADAVAL,* Daughter to *Louis de Lorraine, PRINCE de LAMBESC,* & the Widow of *Dom Jaime Alvares Pereira de Mello, the Third DUKE of CADAVAL.* We can only ſurmiſe that the Ducheſs lay'd her Plan of Seduction after ſhe had been told of the Captain's Proweſs in naval Exploits during the War of *Jenkins' Ear,* & at *Cartagena,* & of his conqueſts of many Ladies, amongſt whom are the much-admir'd Miſs ELIZABETH CHUDLEIGH, & countleſs Beauties of *Naples, Leghorn, Genoa* & *Liſbon.*

Charitable Benefactions Requeſted for the FOUNDLING HOSPITAL.

We take this Opportunity to ſing the Praiſes of the late Captain THOMAS CORAM's *Foundling Hoſpital.*

Capt. CORAM

This worthy & uſeful Inſtitution in Bloomſbury has taken in the unwanted & abandon'd Children of the Poor & Indigent ſince the Year 1745, & ſeeks your Aſſitance in continuing its good Works. We hear *Mr. JONAS HANWAY* has given the moſt generous Sum of £50 to this NOBLE CAUSE.

Several of our fineſt Artiſts diſplay their Works & Converſation Pieces at the Hoſpital, including *Mr. THOMAS GAINSBOROUGH* of *Suffolk,* & the celebrated Mr. WILLIAM HOGARTH, & of late it has become what might be call'd our Nation's firſt Publick Gallery.

In the Chapel, Viſitors may view Mr. HANDEL's magnificent Organ, preſented by that eſtimable Compoſer, which has been employ'd annually ſince 1750 in Hoſpital Performances of his rever'd & ſacred Grand *Oratorio,* The Meſſiah, raiſing £6,725 for the charitable Eſtabliſhment. *Mr. Hogarth* engraves the Tickets from his own ingenious Deſigns.

Remarks upon AUTHORS, & Their BOOKS LATELY PUBLISH'D.

The much-anticipated *Dictionary of the English Language* by *SAMUEL JOHNSON, A.M.,* was publish'd to great Acclaim on the 15th Day of April, & its First Run of Two Thousand Editions has already been fold in its entirety. The Work could be bought for 10s., is prefented in Two Volumes amounting to 2,300 Pages, & weighs an aftonifhing 20*lbs.*

Its Author boafts that he has achiev'd what the joint labour of Forty *Academicians could not produce in a neighbouring Nation in lefs than Half a Century.* Yet feveral purchafers have exprefs'd fome Confufion concerning fundry Omiffions & Errors. While he has included & defin'd *Arfe, Bitch, Bum, Fart, Pifs,* & *Turd,* he has elected to exclude the coarfeft Words from the Lexicon, & when this was remark'd upon by a circle of Ladies, he gave the reply, *"What, my Dears ! Then you have been looking for them ?"* Another Lady enquir'd of him how he came to miftake *Paftern* for the knee of a Horfe, & with unexpected Candour he reply'd, *"Ignorance, Madam, pure Ignorance."*

An Account of an infamous & fcandalous Career may be had in *The Life & Uncommon Adventures of Captain DUDLEY BRADSTREET,* in which the Author fets out a Memoir of his many ignominious Exploits, to pleafe the Reader's Fancy.

Capt. BRADSTREET was born in *Tipperary, Ireland,* & as a Youth enlifted in the Army, but foon forfook the martial Life to trade as a Linen Merchant & a Brewer. The *Jacobite Stirrings* of 1745 afforded him the Opportunity to work as a Spy, & under the Alias *Captain Oliver Williams,* he gain'd Admiffion to the Pretender & his Circle at Derby, acting under the Aufpices of *His Grace The DUKE of CUMBERLAND.*

The Captain boafts that he was the Inftigator of the ill-fam'd Deceit known as *The BOTTLE CONJUROR,* which many of our Readers will recall was brought off in *January of* 1749. It was advertif'd that an unnam'd Performer would appear upon the Stage at the *Haymarket Theatre,* & place his entire Body into an empty Wine Bottle, to the amazement of the affembl'd Throng. The much-heralded Conjuror fail'd to appear on the allotted Evening, & a terrible Riot enfu'd, during which the Playhoufe was ranfack'd. Both the Manager, Mr. SAMUEL FOOTE, & *The Second DUKE of MONTAGU* – a notorious Practitioner of Japery – fell under fufpicion of being Authors of the Fraud.

The GIN ACT of the Year 1736 prov'd lucrative for Informants, who made unlawful Gin Shops known to the Judiciary, & Capt. Bradftreet capitalif'd upon this Practice himfelf, till he perceiv'd that the very Trade upon which he was fpying offer'd greater pecuniary Advantages. He purchaf'd a Houfe, & put up the Sign of a Cat at his Window. There ran a Pipe under this Cat's Claw, & fottifh paffers-by were entreated to place Coins in the Mouth of the Cat, & whifper *"Pufs ! Give Twopence worth of GIN !"* whereupon a Meafure of that finful Liquor would be difpenf'd to the thirfty Patron. We are not furpris'd to learn that the Captain's ill-gotten yield amounted to £220 in his Firft Month of Bufinefs alone.

VOTARY
of
Venus

We prefent to our Readers our bold *Cyprian* for the Month of December, Mi/s FANNY MURRAY.

Renown'd for her Coral-red lips, Cheftnut-brown Treffes, & the perfect Oval of her beauteous Face, Mifs MURRAY has excited the Fancies of many notable Gentlemen. From the Moment of her Firft Seduction when Twelve Years of Age, by the *Hon.* JOHN SPENCER M.P., Grandfon of the *Firft DUKE of MARLBOROUGH*, fhe embark'd upon a Life of Venery, & her inclufion fome Years ago in the *Pimp-General* HARRIS's *LIST of COVENT-GARDEN LADIES* fet her upon a Courfe to greater Advantages. She was kept by Mr. RICHARD *Beau* NASH while at *Bath*, & both the *Fourth EARL of SANDWICH*, & the late Sir RICHARD ATKINS have delighted in her many Charms.

Gallants of the Town who would court her Attentions will be difmay'd to learn that fhe fhall be join'd in Matrimony to the Actor Mr. DAVID ROSS. The Match is arrang'd by EARL SPENCER, fon of the aforemention'd John Spencer, to make amends for his Father's original defpoiling of Mifs Murray, & he has fettl'd upon Mr. Rofs an Allowance of £200 *per annum.*

This Day was publifh'd, Price 2s. 6d.
HARRIS's LIST OF Covent-Garden Ladies:
OR
The MAN of PLEASURE's KALENDAR,

Being an exact Defcription of the moft celebrated Ladies of Pleafure who frequent COVENT-GARDEN, & other Parts of LONDON, & containing Particulars of their Places of Abode, Ages, Hiftories, State of Health, & the Prices afk'd for the Enjoyment of their Favours.

From the fam'd Regifter of Ladies in the keeping of *Mr. Jack Harris, the Pimp-General of All England.*

Printed for H. RANGER, *Temple-Exchange Paffage, Fleet-Street,* & Sold at *The Shakefpear's Head, Covent-Garden,* & at the *Bawdy-houfe of Mother Jane Douglas,* hard by.

Of the CURIOUS HABITS & OPINIONS of Mr. JONAS HANWAY,

With Some Remarks Upon his UMBRELLA, & His Difpute With Mr. SAMUEL JOHNSON A.M.

We are uncertain whether the Contraption employ'd of late by noted Author & Philanthropift Mr. JONAS HANWAY will find favour with the *Bon Ton.*

The Contrivance is known as an UMBRELLA, & is a kind of collapfible Canopy, which guards its owner from Rain. Mr. Hanway fuffers much Raillery from Coach-drivers & Chair-men, who fear they fhall lofe Trade on inclement Days if the Machine is adopted by the Quality. The *Umbrella* – or PORTABLE ROOF – is a common Spectacle in *Paris,* & Mr. Hanway is oft affail'd with cries of *"Frenchman ! Why do you not call a Coach ?"* We underftand Mr. Hanway firft took up an *Umbrella* while travelling in Perfia, where they are uf'd widely. The maroon'd Mariner of Daniel Defoe's popular Novel, *The Life & Surprizing Adventures of Robinfon Crufoe,* fafhion'd fuch a Device for himfelf from Pelts ; hence they are known as *Robinfons,* both here & in France.

Mr. Hanway's *ESSAY on TEA* has elicited much Debate. The Work is an Attack upon that popular Beverage, the high coft & protracted Preparation of which, he believes, are deleterious to the Poor, & to the Nation's Productivity.

This *Flatulent Liquor* – as he terms it – in his Opinion fhortens the Lives of many, rivals Gin in its injurioufnefs, causes paralytic & nervous Diforders, & renders Women ugly. He afferts that the Indigent fquander their Wages upon Tea, & leave their Children to ftarve, which refults in a Decline in the Workforce, & leaves our Army with too few men to defend the Nation in our prefent War againft foreign Foes. There can be no doubt that the Quality of the Beverage confum'd by the Poor is highly queftionable, & that many Vendors peddle Tea fabricated from dry'd leaves of Blackthorn, often with admixtures of naufeous & poifonous Subftances which counterfeit the Appearance of Green Tea.

The celebrated Mr. SAMUEL JOHNSON has engag'd in a War of Words with Mr. Hanway over his animadverfions upon Tea. Mr. Johnson has attack'd & ridicul'd Mr. Hanway & his Writings mercileffly, & avers that for Twenty Years he has relifh'd the Infufion of that fragrant Leaf, with which he has amuf'd his Evenings, folac'd his Midnights, & welcom'd his Mornings. Acrimonious rejoinders have been iffu'd & anfwer'd publickly, & the delivery of Writs is threaten'd.

Dr. CHARLES WHITE &
The UNBURY'D CORPSE of His BENEFACTRESS.

We hear many Narratives of dubious Veracity concerning the inadvertent Burial of seemingly deceas'd yet still-living Unfortunates, but we have never learn'd of zealous Preventatives against such a Horror to equal those employ'd by the late Miss HANNAH BESWICK of *Birchen Bower*, in Oldham, in the County of *Lancashire*.

Till her Death in *February* of this Year, Miss Beswick was a Patron of Dr. CHARLES WHITE, who is the Founder of the Royal Infirmary of *Manchester*. It is rumour'd that Miss Beswick's dear Brother had once reviv'd himself after he had been pronounc'd dead & lay'd in his Coffin, & that this engender'd an abiding Fear in the Lady that the same Fate might befall her. To this effect, she bequeath'd Dr. White the sum of £25,000 by her will, & left him the plainest Instruction that on her passing, she should on no Account be bury'd for One Hundred Years, & that once annually her Body should be inspected, in the presence of Two Witnesses, for any Intimations of Life heretofore absent.

Dead on the Hour!

Perhaps venturing beyond the conditions of his Charge, Dr. White has embalm'd Miss Beswick's mortal remains, & has plac'd her in the empty case of a Clock, so that she might be view'd by Visitors, alongside the Bones of THOMAS HIGGINS, an infamous Highwayman. News of this latest *Specimen* in the anatomickal *Museum* of Dr. White having spread, Miss Beswick is inspected very often by curious Callers, tho' not, we feel bound to remark, in the manner she would have wish'd.

Of the INFAMOUS MORTALITY at the *FOUNDLING HOSPITAL.*

The Plan of Admiſſion adopted in recent Years by the *FOUNDLING HOSPITAL* is now ſeen by all as a Scandalous Failure, & the Shame & Magnitude of the reſultant mortality rate is now uncover'd, to univerſal Condemnation.

Of the 14,934 Children taken into that Charitable Eſtabliſhment ſince the new Scheme was inſtituted, barely 4,400 Souls have ſurviv'd, to the eternal Diſgrace of the Governor, Mr. JONAS HANWAY, & others. The Hoſpital became the Author of its own Woes when it elected to hang a Baſket from its Gates, wherein any Mother might place her child, & ring for a Porter, before taking to her heels. It is alſo generally believ'd that the untramell'd Acceptance of ſo many unwanted Infants by the Hoſpital is encouraging women of looſe & abandon'd Principles into Proſtitution. *His Majeſty's Government* has ſever'd all ties with the Hoſpital, having ſquander'd £500,000 of the Publick's Money upon a Syſtem which has done little more than ſwell the *Bills of Mortality.*

Mr. JONAS HANWAY

PUBLIC CONDEMNATION

The GALLOWS of TYBURN, To Become Moveable.

Whereas the TYBURN GALLOWS, or *Triple Tree,* is an Obſtacle to the Paſſage of Carriage & Horſe in *Mayfair,* it is this Day order'd that it ſhall be taken down, & a moveable Gallows is to be employ'd in its ſtead. This ſhall be kept at *Newgate,* & erected at *Tyburn* only upon thoſe Occaſions when its dread uſe is requir'd.

The Celebrated BLACKAMOOR & MAN of TASTE, Mr. IGNATIUS SANCHO, & His THEORY of MUSICK, Lately Publiſh'd.

Mr. IGNATIUS SANCHO's *Theory of Muſick* is a Work of ſingular Senſibility, & has done much to encreaſe the ſtanding of its Author. It is dedicated to Her Highneſs The PRINCESS ROYAL, who is pleaſ'd to receive it, & perhaps no Scribe or Muſician has tranſcended ſuch baſe & inauſpicious beginnings as thoſe ſuffer'd by Mr. Sancho.

Mr. Sancho was born aboard a Slave-ſhip, during its Paſſage to the *Weſt Indies,* his Mother expiring ſoon thereafter, & his Father dying by his own Hand, rather than ſubmit to a Life of Servitude. The Child was baptiz'd & nam'd *Ignatius* by a Biſhop in thoſe dominions, & he was return'd to *England* when Two Years of Age. Here he became the property of Three Siſters, reſiding at *Greenwich,* who refuſ'd him all Education & Inſtruction.

He was chanc'd upon by *His Grace, the late DUKE* of MONTAGU, who was greatly pleaſ'd with the Boy's Intellect, & took a paternal intereſt in his Nurturing, allowing him to make free with the Books in his Library. His Grace's entreaties to the Siſters to furniſh the Child with Schooling fell upon deaf ears, yet when the Duke departed this Life in the Year 1749, the young Mr. Sancho fled his Three Miſtreſſes, & was given the Poſition of Butler by His Grace's Widow. Upon her demiſe in the Year 1751, ſhe bequeath'd an Annuity of £30 *per annum* upon Mr. Sancho, who of late has aſtounded all with his talent for Muſick, the breadth of his learning, & the readineſs of his Wit. We commend his Book to our Readers.

CROWQUILL

BOSWELL & JOHNSON

PART the SECOND
1760-1769

After a Decade of publishing my Periodickal, I felt settl'd in the Trade I had chosen to pursue. I flatter myself that I had a nose for Gossip, & by the Year of Our Lord Seventeen Hundred & Sixty, Sales were quite excellent. The Publick's appetite for Scandal & Oddities seem'd insatiable, & the People of Quality enjoy'd nothing more than to read about Themselves. I had come to know everyone, & everyone had come to know me.

The News-sheets at this time so excited general Curiosity that it pleas'd some of London's most celebrated Authors to submit Artickles to their Editors on the understanding that their Identities should not become common currency. I do not think I reveal too much if I remark that the esteem'd *Dr. SAMUEL JOHNSON* himself, & his Friend & Biographer *Mr. JAMES BOSWELL*, both wrote for the Presses anonymously, or conceal'd by an *Alias*. In the Year 1761, a well-connected Man of Letters approach'd me with regard to writing regular Paragraphs for my *Gazette* concerning the Exploits of the *Bon Ton*. Honour forbids me to reveal his Name, & he was known to our Readers only as *The SEVEN-DIALS STROLLER*, since he frequented the Purlieus of *London's Seven-Dials* in pursuit of Scandal, Recreation & low Company. His Contributions were consider'd most diverting, & we encreas'd our Patronage greatly as a consequence.

I should like to say that I was able to depend upon my Engraver, *Mr. JAKES*, to fulfil *his* duties with equal Alacrity, but this was not the case. In the Year 1763, he marry'd a spindle-shank'd *Threepenny Upright* call'd *MEG DOXY*, but this cozening harlot soon grew weary of his ill Humours, Indolence, & unwholesome feet. She pilfer'd what little Money & valuables he kept in their *Covent-Garden* attick, prior to absconding with an Offal-seller nam'd *FLANGE*, leaving Jakes with naught but unhappy remembrances & a stubborn Itch. In his unconquerable Melancholy, Mr. Jakes became ever more attach'd to *St. Giles's* Ale-houses, & I was often oblig'd to wrench him from the tavern & to restore him to a state of Sobriety with Coffee & victuals if I wish'd to drag any work from the ungrateful wretch. His language on these Occasions was not fit to be dwelt upon here, & had it not been for his undoubted Talent, & obligation to work to discharge his many Debts to me, I should have consider'd employing the services of another Artist. You might hazard that I am too much of Kindness & Charity.

I am pleas'd to record that the great volume of Advertisements, plac'd in the pages of my *Gazette* by tradesmen, merchants, & Mountebanks, brought in much welcome Revenue, & led happily to a renew'd acquaintance with *Dr. SHINSAW*. My erstwhile Mentor had left His Majesty's Service, & establish'd himself as a Physician in our City, selling to our Patrons his *Nostrum* for Venereal Taints – known as *Shinsaw's Sovereign ELECTUARY* – via our *Gin-Lane* premises. This prov'd a most lucrative Bargain.

The first Year of this new Decade saw a sudden proliferation of Attacks upon Citizens by *MAD DOGS*, & on this account much Fear & Consternation was spread through the Populace of *London*. ——————

The Gin-Lane Gazette

PUBLISHED in LONDON   September, 1760.   Nathaniel Crowquill Esq.

Of the BARBAROUS MEASURES againſt MAD DOGS, lately ſanction'd.

By N. Crowquill, EDITOR.

THERE having been great Miſchiefs done lately in *LONDON* by many MAD DOGS, & the alarm of the Publick not being like very ſoon to ſubſide, the City's *COMMON-COUNCIL* has inſtituted expedients to addreſs the Predicament, tho' we feel ſure that theſe Meaſures ſhall be condemn'd as licenſ'd Cruelty by all who love & revere the Faithful & Innocent amongſt thoſe Creatures. We have been made aware of ſeveral fearful Incidents, & with a pure regard to Truth, relate them here.

Laſt *Thurſday* a mad dog bit a Child on the hand in the *Strand,* & her Parents had her arm immediately cut off to prevent the Infection ſpreading, but the Unfortunate expir'd ſoon after in great Agony.

On *Sunday* Morning laſt, a Mr. WILLIAM HAMBLY of *Deptford* was getting into his Coach,

REWARD

Two Shillings
For the Capture & Killing of
MAD DOGS
By Order of the COMMON-COUNCIL of the
City of LONDON, 26th of Auguſt, 1760.

when he was bit by a mad dog, which had come running down *But-lane,* from the *London Road.* The alarm being raiſ'd, the dog was ſhot ſoon after, cloſe to the Turnpike.

A Girl of *Virginia-ſtreet, Wapping,* of Nine Years of age, was bit by a puppy. On *Monday* laſt, ſhe began to run mad, & her Parents were oblig'd

to tie her down to her bed, & on *Thurſday* ſhe rav'd & bark'd like a dog.

On Sunday night laſt, there died the Son of one Lambert, a Ticket Porter of *Thames-ſtreet.* He was bit by a dog, which alarm'd him terribly, but as there appear'd to be no ſigns of Madneſs about him, his Death is attributed rather to the Fright than to the Wound itſelf.

We alſo hear that a mad dog bit Three other dogs in *Iſlington,* & alſo Two cows belonging to a Mr. Pullein.

On the 26th Day of laſt Month was iſſu'd the Order by *Common-Council* that a Reward of 2s. ſhould be granted for each dog kill'd, & we are outrag'd to ſee every Boy, Apprentice, & nefarious Youth now going about the City carrying clubs & cudgels, with the foul & contemptible Purpoſe of butchering numberleſs dogs defultorily, & for pecuniary gain. We are oblig'd to publiſh the Order in full :-

---

A COMMON-COUNCIL holden in the Chamber
Of the *Guildhall* of the City of LONDON, on Tueſday the 26th Day of
Auguſt, 1760, *Reſolv'd & Order'd*

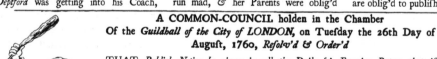

THAT *Publick Notice be given in all the Daily & Evening Papers that if any Dog ſhall be found in the Streets or Highways of the City of London & Liberties thereof, after Wedneſday the 27th Inſtant, for the Space of Two Months, the Conſtables, Beadles of the ſeveral Wards, Watchmen, & other Ward Officers, be directed immediately to KILL ſuch DOG, & this Court will indemnify & ſave harmleſs all Perſons killing ſuch Dogs within the ſaid Time : And that the Conſtables & Beadles of the ſeveral Wards ſhall be entitl'd to & receive Two Shillings from the Deputies of the Wards for every Dog ſo kill'd, & by him bury'd in the Skin, being firſt ſeveral Times ſlaſh'd in the Body. And this Court gives leave to all Perſons whatſoever to bury Dogs on this Occaſion in the Two furthermoſt Quarters of Moorfields from Bethlem.*

Price : Threepence.

INTELLIGENCE in Brief,
from the PROVINCES & Elfewhere.

GALWAY, the 21st Day of *Auguſt.* At *Killkerrin,* near *Moylaigh,* in this County, was marry'd a few days ſince, a young Woman about Twenty-five Years of Age, whoſe Mother about Forty, Grandmother about Eighty, & Great-grandmother of One-hundred & Nine Years, were all preſent. What was moſt ſingular & entertaining was the ſprightlineſs & vivacity with which the latter ſang & danc'd at that advanc'd Age. From her erectneſs of Body, Vigour, & preſent ſeeming State of Health, it is more than probable that ſhe may live to ſee her Fifth & Sixth Generation.

At YORK Races, the 22nd Day of *Auguſt,* a Mr. JOHNSON rode One Mile for 100 Guineas, ſtanding upright on horſeback. He was allow'd Three Minutes in which to achieve this Feat, but perform'd it in Two Minutes & Forty-two Seconds.

At HOLBEACH, the 29th Day of *Auguſt,* a Miſs MARY HAZELL, a young Woman, & ſervant to a Gentleman there, ſent a little Boy to a ſhop for an Ounce of white Mercury, which ſhe ſaid was to poiſon Rats, but took the whole amount herſelf, & expir'd in great Agony the ſame Evening. 'Tis thought ſhe was driven to this by breach of a Promiſe of Marriage.

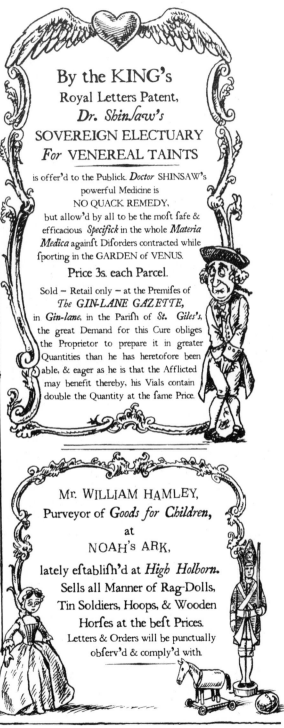

The Gin-Lane Gazette

PUBLISHED in LONDON — *November, 1760.* — Nathaniel Crowquill Esq.

PARTICULARS Concerning the BURSTING of
His Late Majesty The KING's HEART, while engag'd at his CLOSE-STOOL.

By N. Crowquill, Editor.

Ach! Mein Gott! I die on the Throne!

HAVING made several Enquiries of eminent Ladies & Gentlemen of the Court, & Servants of the Royal Houſehold, we are now able to preſent to our Readers a full Account of the unhappy & ſudden demiſe of *His Late Majeſty, KING GEORGE the Second.*

Royal Phyſicians, upon examining his Body, ascertain'd that a *Ventricle* of the King's Heart had burſt, which accounted for the noiſe heard by the Valet while in the next room.

*T*he Hon. HORACE WALPOLE has, we feel, expreſs'd moſt decorouſly & ſuccinctly the views of an entire Nation with the following Eulogy to His Late Majeſty :-

The KING was reſiding at *Kenſington Palace* on the 25th Day of *October,* & aroſe at Six O'Clock that Morning to take a cup of Chocolate, as was his Cuſtom. At a Quarter paſt Seven O'Clock, he was compell'd to anſwer the call of Nature, & took to his Cloſe-ſtool. His Valet heard much ſtraining, follow'd by a terrible *popping* noiſe (which was ſaid to be louder than His *Majeſty's* royal Wind), then a Thud, & finally, a Moan. The Valet ruſh'd to attend the King, & found him lying upon the Floor, with a cut on his Face, which he ſuſtain'd while falling againſt the edge of a Bureau.

His *Majeſty* was carry'd to his Bed, & his royal Daughter, *Princeſs AMELIA,* was ſent for, but the King had expir'd before the moment of her arrival.

WHAT an enviable Death ! In the greateſt Period of the Glory of this Country, and of his Reign, in perfect Tranquillity at home, at Seventy-ſeven, growing blind and deaf, to die without a Pang.

The King's Will ſtipulates that he ſhould be interr'd beſide his beloved late Wife, Queen CAROLINE, & that a ſide of each of their Coffins ſhould be remov'd, in order that the duſt of their mortal Remains ſhould mingle & unite in Death.

Price: Threepence

Of the Popular
NARRATIVE of the LIFE of Mrs. CHARLOTTE CHARKE,
the Breeches Player.

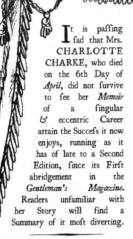

It is paffing fad that Mrs. CHARLOTTE CHARKE, who died on the 6th Day of *April*, did not furvive to fee her *Memoir* of a fingular & eccentric Career attain the Succefs it now enjoys, running as it has of late to a Second Edition, fince its Firft abridgement in the *Gentleman's Magazine*. Readers unfamiliar with her Story will find a Summary of it moft diverting.

Mrs. Charke was Daughter to the late Mr. COLLEY CIBBER, the Actor & *quondam* Poet Laureate, & enjoy'd a wide Education at the beheft of that Gentleman, which took in the *Latin & Italian* Languages. Always a mettlefome & precocious Child, fhe taught herfelf how to groom Horfes, & to fhoot a Firearm. At the Age of Thirteen Years, fhe eftablifh'd a medickal Practice, tho' this endeavour was curtail'd by her Father when he receiv'd confiderable Reckonings for the coftly Phyfick fhe had adminifter'd to her Patrons.

Her indulgent Father uf'd his connexions to affift her in purfuing a Career upon the Stage, & fhe was marry'd to Mr. RICHARD CHARKE, an Actor of Mr. Cibber's circle. Following a Difpute with her Father, Mrs. Charke fet up a theatrickal Company to rival his, & began to take on thofe male Roles for which fhe became renown'd, the part of *Roderigo* in *The Tragedy of Othello* being amongft the moft celebrated.

In the Year 1737, Mr. HENRY FIELDING ftag'd his work *Pafquin*, in which Mrs. Charke took the Role of her own Father. Mr. Cibber's poetick Failings were mock'd remorfelefsly in the Play, leading to a final & irreparable eftrangement between Parent & Daughter.

The Government was quick to note the fatirickal Nature of the work, & as a confequence pafs'd the *Stage Licenfing Act*, which forbids the running of Theatres without a royal Patent. Mr. Richard Charke found himfelf bereft of Employment, & abfconded to *Jamaica*, abandoning Charlotte and their Daughter, Catherine, to the caprice of *Fortune*. Mrs. Charke took on *Punch's Theatre* in *St. James's*, & put on fatirickal Performances of Puppetry, which gib'd at Parliament & the *Bon Ton*, & which circumvented the *Licenfing Act* owing to the abfence of Human Actors upon the ftage. Mrs. Charke's Debts foon overtook her, however, & fhe

fold the Premifes. Her avoidance of Debtors' Gaol was due folely to the pecuniary Generofity of *Covent-garden's* fallen Sifterhood, & Coffee-houfe Proprietors. At this Time, fhe had taken to arraying herfelf almoft habitually in men's Cloaths, & to affociating with her boon Companion, Mrs. BROWN. Difguif'd as a Man, fhe took to her heels to efcape her Creditors, before fecuring employment, firft as Valet to the Rake & Bigamift, the EARL *of* ANGLESEY, & thereafter as a Saufage-maker.

She return'd to *London* & the Stage in the Year 1742, & took a Role in her own Play, *Tit for Tat*, tho' the Work did not prove fuccefsful. Fleeing Debts once more, fhe fill'd feveral Pofitions, which comprif'd thofe of Paftry-cook, Farmer of *Chepftow*, Proof-reader to a *Briftol* News-fheet, & Prompter at the *Orchard-ftreet Theatre* in the City of *Bath*.

Mrs. Charke return'd to London yet again in the Year 1754, & refolv'd to live by her Writing. While her Novel, *The Hiftory of Mr. HENRY DUMONT & Mifs CHARLOTTE EVELYN*, did not yield the Riches fhe crav'd, her own Memoir has prov'd a great Succefs for her Publifher, tho' its placatory Paragraphs did not reconcile her to her Father, as fhe doubtlefs hop'd it fhould. Mrs. Charke died in penury at her Lodgings in the *Haymarket*, at the Age of Forty-feven Years.

The SEVEN DIALS STROLLER

LORD MELCOMBE Breeches *Etiquette.*

Egad ! what an egregious Booby Mr. GEORGE BUBB DODINGTON prov'd himfelf to be, when lately ennobl'd as Baron MELCOMBE of *Melcombe Regis* ! It is remarkable, is it not, how the moft aufpicious of Occafions can take on the moft farcickal Afpects ?

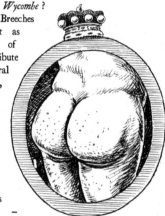

George – the corpulent *Fool* – was found admiring his new Robes vain glorioufly before a Looking-glafs, while practifing Attitudes and difputing with himfelf upon the moft becoming manner of carrying his Coronet. He furpafs'd this abfurdity when, in the act of kneeling to *Her Majefty* QUEEN CHARLOTTE, *his Breeches broke loofe from their Moorings in a moft unbecoming manner*, difcovering a greater ARSE than was ever prefented to the eyes of Royalty !

Is it creditable that I do the old Sinecurift a grave Differvice ? Might it be that Lord Melcombe was honouring a noble Wager, contracted with his fellow Adherents to that Hellfire Club known as the Brotherhood of *St. Francis of Wycombe* ? Or were his Breeches fet at Half-maft as fome manner of unfeafonable Tribute to the late Admiral B Y N G , whom George defended laudably yet unfuccefsfully in *Parliament*, and who was executed – in *Monfieur* AROUET *de* VOLTAIRE's immortal phrafe – *pour encourager les autres* ? I leave it to my dear Readers to determine.

Baron MELCOMBE   **His ARSE**

To the EDITOR.

SIR,

I HAD the great good Fortune to attend the Banquet at the *Guildhall on Lord Mayor's Day*, the 16th of *November*, and witneſſ'd the riotous and infamous Attack by the ferocious Mob, there aſſembl'd. There can be little doubt that the young KING's unwarrantable partiality towards his deſpiſ'd Secretary of State, *Lord* BUTE, was the *primum mobile* of this OUTRAGE.

H*is Majeſty's* Coach was obſerv'd by the Throng in ſilence, but that of Lord Bute was harangu'd with cries of *No Bute* ! and was ſet upon by vengeful and deſperate People. His Lordſhip made good his Eſcape, due only to the ſwift actions of his Guard of Prize-fighters and Butchers, which now ſeems to accompany his every Publick Engagement.

U pon the arrival of Mr. Pitt, the ſtreets and balconies burſt into deafening Cheers, and cries of *Pitt for ever* ! went up, the Ladies all the while waving their Handkerchiefs, and the Mob graſping at the Coach's wheels, ſhaking hands with the Footmen, and kiſſing the Horſes. Mr. Pitt was greeted at the Guildhall by loud *Huzzas* and Applauſe from the very Magiſtrates of the City ! Never before has your Correſpondent ſeen the like. Mr. Pitt's popularity with the bellicoſe Citizenry in ſetting himſelf at defiance againſt the pacifick Inclinations of *His Majeſty* and *His Lordſhip*, in reſpect of the vexatious matter of the War's continuance or curtailment, muſt ſurely have ſpurr'd the People's actions.

Yours &c.
T.W., *Cheapſide.*

Of the late HAUNTINGS by SCRATCHING FANNY of COCK-LANE, with fome Remarks upon the ENQUIRY into their AUTHENTICITY.

By N. Crowquill, EDITOR.

THE Conjecture & publick *Delirium* furrounding the putative GHOST now refiding in *Cock-lane* continues unabated. Your Editor feels it his duty to fet before his Readers the Facts of the Cafe as they now ftand, that they might fettle in their own Minds whether events to date betoken the Manifeftation of a *bona fide* preternatural Agency, or whether they are a DESPICABLE IMPOSTURE & a DECEITFUL CONTRIVANCE, perpetrated by the loweft Cafte of avaricious Charlatans & iniquitous SCOUNDRELS.

One Mr. RICHARD PARSONS, a Parifh Clerk, furnifh'd one Mr. WILLIAM KENT of *Norfolk* with Lodgings at his Houfe in *Cock-lane*, in St. Sepulchre's, Two Years hence. Mr. Kent was in the company of one FANNY LYNES, his Sifter-in-Law, with whom he had become intimate fince the Demife of his Firft Wife, Elizabeth Lynes. Not long after Mr. Kent & Mifs Lynes took up their new Refidence, Mr. Parfons borrow'd the fum of 12 *Guineas* from Mr. Kent, which foon became a well-fpring of Contention betwixt the Two Men.

Mr. Kent being call'd away on Bufinefs, Fanny invited Mr. Parfons's young Daughter, ELIZABETH – of whom fhe had become very fond – to fhare her bed. In the dead of Night, they were ftarted from their fleep by ftrange fcratching noifes in the Wainfcoting, & Fanny felt certain that the Shade of her late Sifter was vifiting her for fome fearful Purpofe. Upon his return, Mr. Kent found his *Inamorata* quite befide herfelf with nervous Diftraction.

Mr. Kent's demand for the fettlement of his Loan to Mr. Parfons being refuf'd, & blackmail concerning the former's *Fornication* with Fanny being threaten'd by the Clerk, the Lovers remov'd themfelves from *Cock-lane*, & fecur'd Lodgings elfewhere. It is fad to report that very fhortly thereafter, on the 2nd Day of *February*, 1760, Fanny died of the Small-pox, & was interr'd at *St. John's Church, Clerkenwell.*

Mr. Kent continu'd to infift upon Remuneration from Mr. Parfons, who counter'd thefe Demands with Claims that the unearthly fcratching, banging, & knocking Noifes had refum'd in his Houfe, & that they were made by the Spectre of late Fanny Lynes. Parfons averr'd that her Spirit had inform'd him that Mr. Kent had poifon'd her by adminiftering Arfenic mix'd with Purl which Mr. Kent has moft vociferoufly deny'd.

The Hon. HORACE WALPOLE & His Grace The DUKE of YORK call upon SCRATCHING FANNY, but find her ABSENT.

THE Haunting has excited the Curiofity of many of Rank & Character. The Houfe was lately vifited by *His Grace the* DUKE *of* YORK, the *Hon.* HORACE WALPOLE, *Lady* NORTHUMBERLAND, *Lady* MARY COKE, & *Lord* HERTFORD, who made up a Party after attending the *Opera*, to drive to *Cock-lane.*

The Lane being much congefted with the Mob, the Worthies were unable at firft to gain admittance, yet when it was perceiv'd by the People that His Grace was of the Company, they were allow'd Paffage infide. Fifty fouls fill'd the Child's hot & ftinking Bed-chamber, which was lighted by but one Tallow-candle. The Affembly was inform'd that the Ghoft would not come until 7 O'Clock in the Morning, & the Duke & his fcornful Companions departed the Houfe at Half an Hour paft One.

News of the fuppos'd Haunting foon fpread, & the Ale-houfes of the Parifh have capitalif'd greatly upon the Influx of curious & thirfty Vifitors. The Citizenry & enthufiaftick *Methodifts* now gather in great Numbers to witnefs an acquaintance of Mr. Parfons, one MARY FRASER, put Enquiries to the Ghoft, & to hear the Replies it gives by knocking once to anfwer in the affirmative, & twice in the negative. All the while, the Parfons Child repofes in her Bed, while the Ghoft & its Interlocutor converfe clamoroufly in the abovemention'd manner. The young Mifs Parfons fays that fhe feels the Spirit like a *Moufe upon her back.*

At the beheft of the *Lord Mayor,* Sir SAMUEL FLUDYER, an Enquiry into the bufinefs has been arrang'd by the Reverend STEPHEN ALDRICH of *Clerkenwell,* to afcertain whether the Ghoft's exiftence, & its Allegations againft Mr. Kent, fhould be given any credence. The Ghoft, it feems, has affented to this Propofal. On this head, an Affemblage of Seven eminent Worthies fhall gather, in the dead of Night, in the Crypt of *St. John's Church,* & the late Mifs Fanny Lynes fhall anfwer their Queftions by knocking againft the lid of her Coffin. Not fince the bafe & fraudulent Trickery of the *Bottle Conjuror* has fuch a metaphyfical Conundrum impof'd itfelf upon fo bewilder'd a Publick.

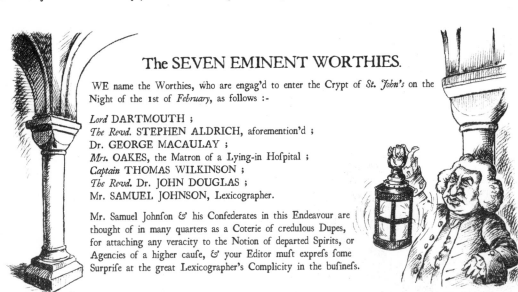

The SEVEN EMINENT WORTHIES.

WE name the Worthies, who are engag'd to enter the Crypt of *St. John's* on the Night of the 1st of *February,* as follows :-

Lord DARTMOUTH ;
The Revd. STEPHEN ALDRICH, aforemention'd ;
Dr. GEORGE MACAULAY ;
Mrs. OAKES, the Matron of a Lying-in Hofpital ;
Captain THOMAS WILKINSON ;
The Revd. Dr. JOHN DOUGLAS ;
Mr. SAMUEL JOHNSON, Lexicographer.

Mr. Samuel Johnfon & his Confederates in this Endeavour are thought of in many quarters as a Coterie of credulous Dupes, for attaching any veracity to the Notion of departed Spirits, or Agencies of a higher caufe, & your Editor muft exprefs fome Surprife at the great Lexicographer's Complicity in the bufinefs.

Particulars concerning Mifs JULIANA POPJOY, *Inamorata* of the late Mr. *BEAU* NASH, now dwelling in a HOLLOW TREE.

GRIEF may manifeſt itſelf in countleſs Forms, yet rarely does it diſquiet a Lady's Mind ſo egregiouſly that ſhe feels compell'd to retire from publick Life, & rarer ſtill does any Lady do ſo in as eccentrick a manner as that ſettl'd upon of late by Mifs JULIANA POPJOY.

The Death on the 3rd Day of *February* of Mr. RICHARD *Beau* NASH, the *Maſter of Ceremonies* at *Bath*, was taken dreadful hard by Mifs Popjoy, tho' their amatory Attachment had ended ſome time before. In his declining Years, Mr. Naſh enjoy'd neither good Health, nor pecuniary *Equilibrium*, ſlave that he was to the Gaming-tables & ſo a reſidence with Mifs Popjoy for a Time was obtruded on him by Neceſſity, yet ſhe was pleaſ'd to take him in. He is now bury'd in a Pauper's Grave.

Mifs Popjoy is ſo diſtraught at Mr. Naſh's Paſſing that ſhe has vow'd to dwell perpetually in a HOLLOW TREE, near the Town of *Warminſter*, & ſleeps only upon Straw within this arboreal Lodge, eſchewing the comforts of a Bed for the remainder of her Days. Upon thoſe occaſions when ſhe ventures to *Briſtol* or *Bath*, ſhe allows herſelf the Indulgence of ſlumbering in a Barn or Out-houſe.

Mifs Popjoy is a former Dreſs-maker, & is known in Bath by the *Sobriquet* Lady BETTY BESOM, as ſhe once own'd & rode a grey Horſe, which ſhe urg'd on with a Whip of many Thongs. We are ſorry to ſee her renounce the World, & to think of the Heart-fetch'd ſighs which emanate from that lonely Tree in *Wiltſhire*.

O Woe! Woe! Woe beyond Endurance!

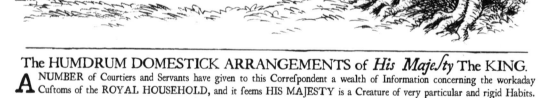

The HUMDRUM DOMESTICK ARRANGEMENTS of *His Majeſty* The KING.

A NUMBER of Courtiers and Servants have given to this Correſpondent a wealth of Information concerning the workaday Cuſtoms of the ROYAL HOUSEHOLD, and it ſeems HIS MAJESTY is a Creature of very particular and rigid Habits.

The KING riſes at Six O'Clock in the Morning, and buſies himſelf with Letters and Miſſives, before enjoying a ſhort Ride. He then joins *Her Majeſty* Queen CHARLOTTE for Breakfaſt, thereafter attending to State

Buſineſs unceaſingly until Four O'Clock of the Afternoon, when he takes Dinner, which uſually compriſes Soup, a plain Joint of Meat, broil'd Fowls, and Pies. Mindful of his girth, he reſtricts himſelf to Fruit Tarts and Grapes for Deſart.

At Seven O'Clock, the King and Queen viſit their royal Children, or call upon the PRINCESS DOWAGER, and in the Seaſon they attend the Theatre, or grand *Oratorios* of *German* Muſick. The royal Supper conſiſts of Broth, Chicken or Turkey, cold Mutton, Eggs, and a Cuſtard, and is ſerv'd at _____

Ods bobs! ENOUGH!
Do you mean to weary our Readers into Inſenſibility?!
N.C., EDITOR.

The SEVEN DIALS STROLLER

Of The EARL of SANDWICH, attack'd by Mr. JOHN WILKES's *BABOON.*

I HAVE often fcandalif'd you with News of the infamous and lewd Practices of Sir FRANCIS DASHWOOD's Hell-fire Club, the *Brotherhood of St. Francis of Wycombe,* yet tho' the old Libertine is appointed *Chancellor of the Exchequer* — a pofition of Refpect and Emolument — he lately allows his fenfualift Confederates even greater Licenfe at *Medmenham* than heretofore reported.

R umour reaches me that the Friars lately perform'd a *Black Mafs,* during which they fcream'd Imprecations at GOD, and dar'd Him to prove His exiftence. Unbeknown to moft of thofe prefent, Mr. JOHN WILKES M.P. had procur'd a BABOON — perhaps from his fellow *Friar,* Sir HENRY VANSITTART, the *Governor of Bengal* — arraying it in a DEVIL's garb, and concealing it in a Cheft kept by the Friars for the purpofes of ftoring the Accoutrements of their diabolical Ceremonies.

T his Cheft was fecur'd with a Spring-lock, to which the fneaking dog Wilkes had tied a Cord, running it under the Carpet to his cuftomary Chair, that he might lay his Hand upon it at an appofite Juncture. Growing weary of the ungodly Ceremony unfolding before him, Wilkes of a fudden releaf'd the Baboon from its Skulking-hole, whereupon it leapt onto the Altar, and then onto the Shoulder of the ftartl'd Fool LORD SANDWICH, who is faid to have addreff'd the Creature

in the following manner : *Spare me, gracious DEVIL ! Spare a Wretch who was never fincerely your Servant ! I have finn'd only from the Vanity of being in Fafhion. I never committed a Thoufandth part of the Vices of which I boafted ! Take fomeone elfe, they are all worfe than I ! I never knew that you'd come !*

T aking pity upon His Lordfhip, one of the Party was able to defeneftrate the Baboon, who fhow'd greater Senfe than his Gaolers in quitting the Scene, and has not been heard of fince.

W ilkes was inveigl'd into this Circle of Voluptuaries by the late Mr. THOMAS POTTER M.P., the Vice-Treafurer of Ireland, who was an Intimate of the bloated Bubb Dodington, and a man fo abandon'd to Vice that he once boafted of fodomifing a Cow on Wingrove-common, in the County of Buckinghamfhire.

Of the COCK-LANE FRAUDSTERS, ### & their forthcoming TRIAL.

W e are happy to report that the bafe Perpetrators of the vile Fraud, known as the COCK-LANE GHOST, will now be brought to book, their Trial being fet for the 10th Day of *July* next. The Company of Gentlemen who vifited the Crypt of *St. John's* on the 1st of February in order to interview *Scratching Fanny* were anfwer'd only with Silence, & concluded that no preternatural Power was evident.

T he PARSONS Child was remov'd to the *Covent-garden* Abode of Mr. DANIEL MISSITER, an Affociate of the *Revd. Stephen Aldrich,* where fhe was obferv'd in fecret on the 21st of *February* to remove from the Hearth a fmall wooden Kettle-ftand, which fhe conceal'd under her Stays & uf'd to make thofe fcratching & knocking founds which are now infamous.

M r. William Kent is proclaim'd entirely innocent of the Crime lay'd to his Charge. The bafe villain, drunkard, & originator of the Deception, *Richard Parfons,* & his Wife, were apprehended. The Ghoft's principal Apologifts, the *Methodift Revd. John Moore,* & *Mr. Charles Say,* the News-fheet Editor, were alfo taken into Cuftody. We truft that Juftice will now take her majeftic & impartial Courfe.

Of Mrs. MARY DARLY's moſt diverting BOOK of CARICATURAS.

THE ART of *CARICATURA* is in High Faſhion with the *Bon Ton*, & it is not merely thoſe who etch & trade in the Print Shops who may now practiſe this *Italian* Amuſement. Lately was publiſh'd *A BOOK of CARICATURAS*, by that moſt talented of Engravers, Mrs. MARY DARLY, who ſtyles herſelf a *Fun Merchant*, & who ſeeks to inſtruct her Readers & Patrons in the Art of drawing & etching their Friends & Relations in their own Parlours.

Mrs. Darly avers that *Caricatura is the moſt diverting Species of Deſigning, that will certainly keep thoſe that practiſe it out of the Hipps or Vapours,* & her Book ſets out, *on Sixty Copper Plates, in that Droll & Pleaſing Manner,* the Methods by which they might ſchool themſelves in this Art.

Mrs. Darly is pleaſ'd to offer Tutelage to young Gentlemen & Ladies, either in perſon or *via* Correſpondence, giving Hints upon Sketches deliver'd to her, Poſt paid. She will alſo etch & print any *Caricatura* from Sketches & written Particulars with which her Patrons ſee fit to furniſh her. She & her Huſband, Mr. MATTHEW DARLY, have indeed progreſſ'd wonderfully in their Trade ſince the unfortunate buſineſs of their being brought to Trial for ſelling lewd & ſeditious Prints, & the MARQUIS of TOWNSHEND is become one of their moſt eſteem'd Patrons. They may be found at the Sign of the Acorn, at *Ryder's-court, Fleet-ſtreet.*

To the EDITOR.
SIR,

ON the 25th Day of this Month, I attended the Opening of *Parliament*, and witneſſ'd the Mob's unwarrantable Actions towards LORD BUTE. He was met with Hiſſes, and Cries of *NO BUTE* ! and *NO SCOTCH ROGUES* ! before

PUTTING *the* BUTE *in,* — — *Or* — JOHN BULL *parleys with the* SCOTCH ROGUE.

ſuffering the Indignity of being pelted with Offal and Mud. There can be little doubt that the Protection afforded by his Company of Prize-fighters was all that ſtood between him and grievous Injury, when his *Hackney-chair* was attack'd, and its glaſs broken. The KING was haraſſ'd alſo, but is perhaps made of ſterner ſtuff than his Scotch Favourite, and attended the Theatre that Evening as he had plann'd.

I have it on good Authority that the cumulative Effects of this now habitual Violence and Ill-uſage, and the flood of ſatirickal Etchings and Squibs which pours forth almoſt daily from the City's Print-ſhops, is driving His Lordſhip to the ineſcapable Judgment that he muſt ſoon relinquiſh his Office. Whether any credence ſhould be granted the current Suppoſition that Lord Bute is the *Paramour* of the PRINCESS DOWAGER, your Correſpondent is not in a poſition to deny or confirm.

I am
Yours &c.,
J. H.
Mayfair.

An OBITUARY ;

With Particulars concerning the Perplexing Cafe of the late MARY TOFTS, who gave Birth to SEVENTEEN RABBITS.

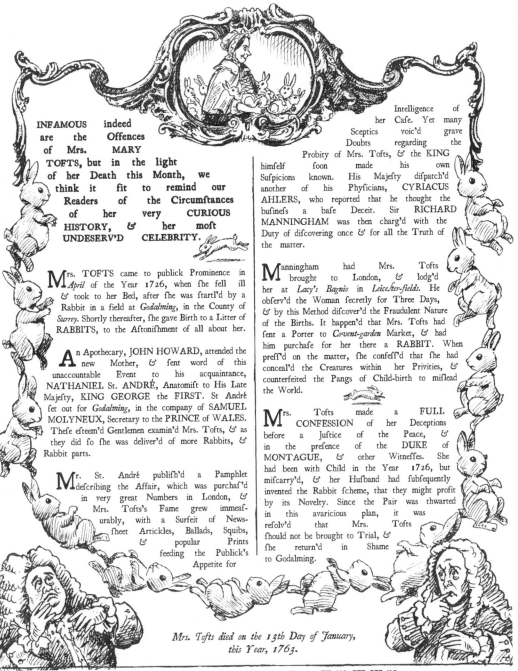

INFAMOUS indeed are the Offences of Mrs. MARY TOFTS, but in the light of her Death this Month, we think it fit to remind our Readers of the Circumftances of her very CURIOUS HISTORY, & her moft UNDESERV'D CELEBRITY.

Mrs. TOFTS came to publick Prominence in *April* of the Year 1726, when fhe fell ill & took to her Bed, after fhe was ftartl'd by a Rabbit in a field at *Godalming*, in the County of *Surrey*. Shortly thereafter, fhe gave Birth to a Litter of RABBITS, to the Aftonifhment of all about her.

An Apothecary, JOHN HOWARD, attended the new Mother, & fent word of this unaccountable Event to his acquaintance, NATHANIEL St. ANDRÉ, Anatomift to His Late Majefty, KING GEORGE the FIRST. St André fet out for *Godalming*, in the company of SAMUEL MOLYNEUX, Secretary to the PRINCE of WALES. Thefe efteem'd Gentlemen examin'd Mrs. Tofts, & as they did fo fhe was deliver'd of more Rabbits, & Rabbit parts.

Mr. St. André publifh'd a Pamphlet defcribing the Affair, which was purchaf'd in very great Numbers in London, & Mrs. Tofts's Fame grew immeafurably, with a Surfeit of Newsfheet Artickles, Ballads, Squibs, & popular Prints feeding the Publick's Appetite for Intelligence of her Cafe. Yet many Sceptics voic'd grave Doubts regarding the Probity of Mrs. Tofts, & the KING himfelf foon made his own Sufpicions known. His Majefty difpatch'd another of his Phyficians, CYRIACUS AHLERS, who reported that he thought the bufinefs a bafe Deceit. Sir RICHARD MANNINGHAM was then charg'd with the Duty of difcovering once & for all the Truth of the matter.

Manningham had Mrs. Tofts brought to London, & lodg'd her at *Lacy's Bagnio* in *Leicefter-fields*. He obferv'd the Woman fecretly for Three Days, & by this Method difcover'd the Fraudulent Nature of the Births. It happen'd that Mrs. Tofts had fent a Porter to *Covent-garden* Market, & had him purchafe for her there a RABBIT. When prefs'd on the matter, fhe confefs'd that fhe had conceal'd the Creatures within her Privities, & counterfeited the Pangs of Child-birth to miflead the World.

Mrs. Tofts made a FULL CONFESSION of her Deceptions before a Juftice of the Peace, & in the prefence of the DUKE of MONTAGUE, & other Witneffes. She had been with Child in the Year 1726, but mifcarry'd, & her Hufband had fubfequently invented the Rabbit fcheme, that they might profit by its Novelty. Since the Pair was thwarted in this avaricious plan, it was refolv'd that Mrs. Tofts fhould not be brought to Trial, & fhe return'd in Shame to Godalming.

Mrs. Tofts died on the 13th Day of January, this Year, 1763.

Of the HALF-PRICE RIOT at the THEATRE ROYAL, *Covent-garden.*

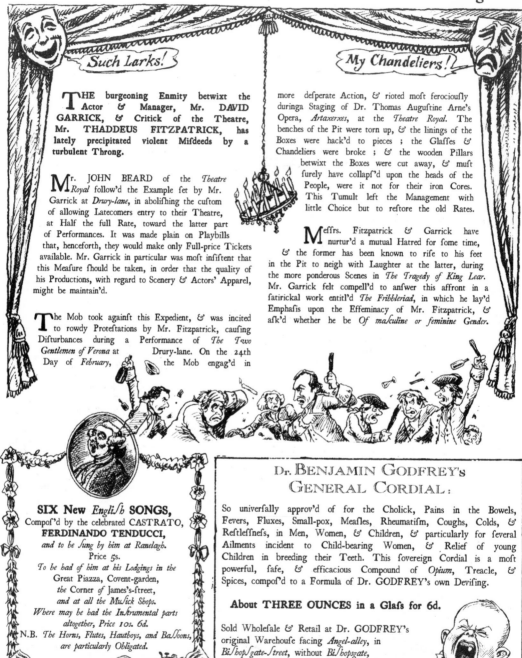

Such Larks!

My Chandeliers!

THE burgeoning Enmity betwixt the Actor & Manager, Mr. DAVID GARRICK, & Critick of the Theatre, Mr. THADDEUS FITZPATRICK, has lately precipitated violent Mifdeeds by a turbulent Throng.

Mr. JOHN BEARD of the *Theatre Royal* follow'd the Example fet by Mr. Garrick at *Drury-lane*, in abolifhing the cuftom of allowing Latecomers entry to their Theatre, at Half the full Rate, toward the latter part of Performances. It was made plain on Playbills that, henceforth, they would make only Full-price Tickets available. Mr. Garrick in particular was moft infiftent that this Meafure fhould be taken, in order that the quality of his Productions, with regard to Scenery & Actors' Apparel, might be maintain'd.

The Mob took againft this Expedient, & was incited to rowdy Proteftations by Mr. Fitzpatrick, caufing Difturbances during a Performance of *The Two Gentlemen of Verona* at Drury-lane. On the 24th Day of *February*, the Mob engag'd in more defperate Action, & rioted moft ferocioufly duringa Staging of Dr. Thomas Auguftine Arne's Opera, *Artaxerxes*, at the *Theatre Royal*. The benches of the Pit were torn up, & the linings of the Boxes were hack'd to pieces ; the Glaffes & Chandeliers were broke ; & the wooden Pillars betwixt the Boxes were cut away, & muft furely have collapf'd upon the heads of the People, were it not for their iron Cores. This Tumult left the Management with little Choice but to reftore the old Rates.

Meffrs. Fitzpatrick & Garrick have nurtur'd a mutual Hatred for fome time, & the former has been known to rife to his feet in the Pit to neigh with Laughter at the latter, during the more ponderous Scenes in *The Tragedy of King Lear*. Mr. Garrick felt compell'd to anfwer this affront in a fatirickal work entitl'd *The Fribbleriad*, in which he lay'd Emphafis upon the Effeminacy of Mr. Fitzpatrick, & afk'd whether he be *Of mafculine or feminine Gender.*

The SEVEN DIALS STROLLER

An Account of the FIRE that claim'd both the LEG of Mifs HENRIETTA MOLESWORTH, & the Life of her MOTHER.

IT is my unenviable tafk to relate to you a fad and troubling Hiftory, redeem'd only by an affecting Inftance of the Human Spirit's Refilience in the face of unexampl'd Misfortune.

At Four O'Clock, on the Morning of the 5th of *May*, there broke out a terrible Fire at the Houfe of LADY MOLESWORTH, in *Grofvenor-Square*. Her Ladyfhip was abed with her Daughter of Sixteen Years — and the *Inamorata* of LORD GROSVENOR — the charming Mifs HENRIETTA MOLESWORTH, when the fearfome Conflagration took hold.

The Flames from the Rooms below crept ever nearer to the Bed-chamber of thefe poor Unfortunates, and Smoak threaten'd to overcome them.

Mifs Henrietta, feeing that no other courfe of Action offer'd itfelf, leapt from their Window, on the Second Floor, dropt onto fharp Railings below, and broke her Leg, before tumbling into the Bafement. Her Mother obferv'd this defperate Feat with inexpreffible Horror, but was unable to emulate her Daughter's Example, through Fear for her own perfon and her youngeft Children in the Nurfery. The Floor upon which fhe ftood fuddenly giving way, fhe fell to a fhocking Death, and was confum'd by the *Inferno*. Her Daughters, Mary and Melofina, were alfo loft.

The Two remaining Sifters hurry'd to the top of the Building, and dropt onto Mattreffes and Feather-beds arrang'd to receive them, by the Crowd affembl'd in the Street. Their Governefs mifjudg'd her leap, and was mangl'd on the Pavement. The charr'd Bones and the Wedding-ring of Lady Molefworth were later difcover'd amongft the fmoaking cinders.

Henrietta was carry'd to LADY GROSVENOR's Houfe, which adjoin'd that of the Molefworths, and a Surgeon was fummon'd. Her Leg was in fuch an injur'd ftate that it had to be cut off above the Knee.

I am given to underftand that Henrietta's Recuperation proceeds well, but fhe is not yet apprif'd of the lofs of her Leg, claiming that fhe feels difcomfort in that Phantom extremity. Her Phyficians have contriv'd a bandag'd falfe Limb to be attach'd to the ftump, *pro tempore*, until an appofite Juncture can be found at which to inform the young Lady of the Truth of the Matter. I am outrag'd by the Intelligence that the difhonourable and fickle-hearted Lord Grofvenor is now on the point of breaking his Attachment to the unhappy young Lady, who is fuftain'd only by the Bleffing of fine Spirits, and an uncommon fhare of Fortitude.

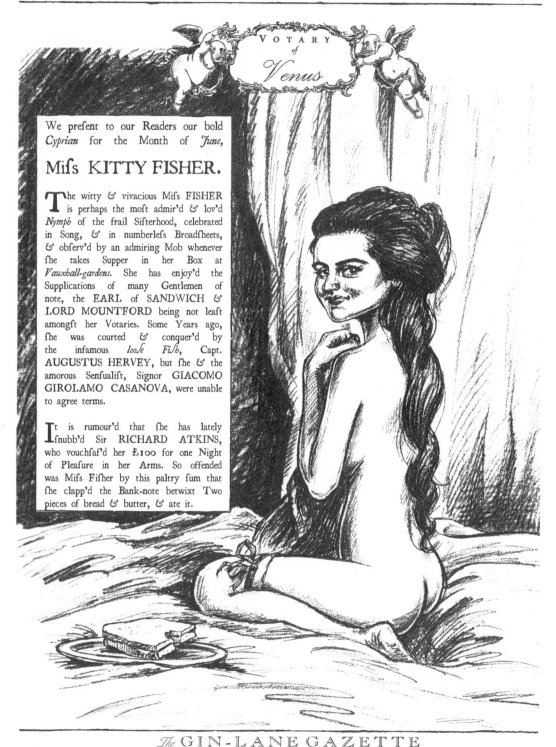

VOTARY
of
Venus

We prefent to our Readers our bold *Cyprian* for the Month of *June,*

Mifs KITTY FISHER.

The witty & vivacious Mifs FISHER is perhaps the moft admir'd & lov'd *Nymph* of the frail Sifterhood, celebrated in Song, & in numberlefs Broadfheets, & obferv'd by an admiring Mob whenever fhe takes Supper in her Box at *Vauxhall-gardens.* She has enjoy'd the Supplications of many Gentlemen of note, the EARL of SANDWICH & LORD MOUNTFORD being not leaft amongft her Votaries. Some Years ago, fhe was courted & conquer'd by the infamous *loofe Fifh,* Capt. AUGUSTUS HERVEY, but fhe & the amorous Senfualift, Signor GIACOMO GIROLAMO CASANOVA, were unable to agree terms.

It is rumour'd that fhe has lately fnubb'd Sir RICHARD ATKINS, who vouchfaf'd her £100 for one Night of Pleafure in her Arms. So offended was Mifs Fifher by this paltry fum that fhe clapp'd the Bank-note betwixt Two pieces of bread & butter, & ate it.

Of the LONDON PEREGRINATIONS of the MOZART FAMILY.

We are happy to note that the Father of the Child Prodigy of Nature, Mafter WOLFGANG MOZART, is now fufficiently recover'd in his Health to allow that Family to quit their *pro tempore* Refidence of Dr. Randal's Houfe at *Five-Fields Row, in Chelfea.* Herr LEOPOLD MOZART fell ill as a confequence of hurrying on Foot behind the Sedan-chair in which his Two Children were carry'd to *Grofvenor-Square,* for the purpofe of performing at the Concert given there by Lord THANET. The Gentleman alfo fat that Evening in a harmful Draught, which furely contributed to his Indifpofition. The younger Mozart has been far from idle during this Sojourn of Seven Weeks, & has written Two *Symphonies.*

We cannot wonder at Herr Mozart's Infirmity, given the endlefs round of Engagements to which he & his Family have pledg'd themfelves fince their Arrival in *London,* in *April.* Wolfgang was prefented to the KING & QUEEN on the 27th of *April,* & accompany'd Her Majefty in a Song on the *Harpfichord.* On the 5th of *June,* both Wolfgang & Maria Anna, his Sifter, perform'd at a grand Concert of Vocal & Inftrumental Mufick at *Spring-garden,* in Honour of the King's Birth-day. Performances have alfo taken place at *Ranelagh-gardens,* & at Charing-crofs. The Mozarts have refided during this Time at *The White Bear Inn, Piccadilly,* at *Cecil-court, St. Martin's-lane,* & at *Chelfea,* as reported above. They now make their Abode in Frith-ftreet, & fhall remain there until their Departure from England next Year.

You're adorable!

Of the INFANT BISHOP of *OSNABRÜCK,* & the Commemoration thereof.

It is announc'd that gold & filver Medals fhall be iffu'd next Year, in commemoration of young Prince FREDERICK's Election to the remunerative Bifhopric of *Ofnabrück.* Our own dear KING is the prefent PRINCE ELECTOR of HANOVER, the Holder of which Title enjoys the Privilege of appointing every alternate Bifhop of that Dominion, & he has chofen to honour his royal Son with the epifcopal Ennoblement. It is perhaps as well that the Pofition is a purely titular one, given that Prince Frederick was only Six Months of Age at the time of his Election, on the 27th Day of *February.*

Of LADY WATSON-WENTWORTH's Scandalous ELOPEMENT with her FOOTMAN.

Lady HENRIETTA WATSON-WENTWORTH has heretofore fhewn the World an unblemifh'd Character, & evinc'd naught but admirable good Senfe, as befits the Sifter of the *Marquefs* of ROCKINGHAM, but fhe has lately brought Difgrace upon her Family's good Name in eloping with her *Irifh* Footman, Mr. JOHN WILLIAM STURGEON.

Mr. Sturgeon, of the Parifh of *St. George,* near *Hanover-Square,* was illiterate when he firft enter'd her Ladyfhip's Service, but fhe made it her particular Concern to tutor him in Grammar, Mathematicks, & Mufick. The unbecoming Intimacy that this Arrangement engender'd betwixt Miftrefs & Hireling muft furely have led to unfeemly Writhings & Rummagings in the Bed-chamber, & to the defperate Expedient of their late Flight.

They are now marry'd, & Lady Watfon-Wentworth appears to have recover'd fome of her Wits in fettling but a fingle £100 *per annum* upon her Hufband, entailing her whole Fortune upon fuch Children as might be born of the Match, with Reverfion to her own Family, & providing that in the Event of their Separation, Sturgeon's Annuity fhould ftill be paid to him. She has given away all her fineft Cloaths, averring that Linen Gowns are more fitting for the Wife of a Footman, & fhe is accompanying her Hufband to *Ireland* to vifit his Family, as plain Mrs. *HENRIETTA STURGEON.*

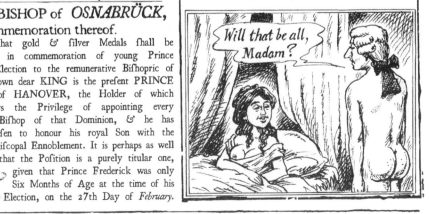

Will that be all, Madam?

Particulars concerning the PETITION of the PERRUQUE-MAKERS to His Majesty The KING.

THE Perruque has for some Time been out of favour with the Quality, & the KING himself wears naught but his own Hair, occasioning those who rely upon the Trade a considerable loss of Revenue. Yet in seeking to improve their Lot, the Perruque-makers have brought much Ridicule upon themselves.

A great Number of these Tradesmen petition'd His Majesty to make the wearing of Perruques by the Gentry a statutory Requirement, & on the 11th Day of *February* a large Company of them proceff'd to *St. James's Palace* to wait upon the King's Pleasure in this Solicitation. His Majesty was pleaf'd to receive them, but graciously declin'd their Entreaties.

The Mob observ'd that the preponderance of the Petitioners were not themselves wearing Perruques &, seizing them, they subjected the Company to rough usage in cutting off their Hair !

The *Hon.* HORACE WALPOLE has enquir'd whether we should wonder if Carpenters were to remonstrate that, since the Peace, there is no demand for wooden Legs, delighting many, once again, with his ready Wit. A satirickal Petition on behalf of the City's Carpenters is lately publish'd, which beseeches the King & his Servants to wear wooden Legs.

Of the TRIAL of the Duellist, LORD BYRON, forthcoming.

THE Date for the Trial of Lord BYRON is now settl'd upon, being the 16th Day of *April* next. His Lordship stands accus'd of the Murder of Mr. WILLIAM CHAWORTH, which is said to have come about in the following Manner :-

Lord Byron & Mr. Chaworth were amongst a Company that din'd one Evening in *January* at the *Star & Garter*, in *Pall-mall*. The celebrated Claret of the House flow'd bounteously, & the Conversation proceeded on convivial terms, until a violent Quarrel broke out betwixt the Two Gentlemen aforemention'd, concerning the merits of the Game kept on their respective Estates. Mr. Chaworth ask'd a Waiter to have a Room set aside, that Honour might be satisfy'd in private.

A candle was plac'd on the Table, the door was fasten'd to prevent interruption, & the Gentlemen drew Swords. During the ensuing Contest, Mr. Chaworth's blade cut Lord Byron's Waistcoat & Shirt for Eight Inches or more, before His Lordship made a Thrust that hit its mark, & prov'd fatal to Mr. Chaworth the following Day.

Lord Byron has asserted his ancient Right to be tried at *Westminster Hall*, in the Presence of Two-hundred & Fifty of his fellow Peers of the Realm. By this Expedient he doubtless seeks to escape a Capital Sentence. He has also donn'd mourning garb, as a mark of Respect — pretended or otherwise — to his late Adversary.

Tickets for the Trial are now sold at 6 Guineas each, & Galleries for the numberless Gentlefolk who wish to attend the Proceedings are under construction in the Hall. There shall also be Two great Boxes cover'd with crimson Cloth, to accommodate the Royal Family & sundry Foreign Ministers.

Particulars concerning the Return to the Stage of Mr. SAMUEL FOOTE, after the Lofs of his FOOT.

OUR Readers will be happy to learn that Mr. SAMUEL FOOTE is now to be feen return'd to the Stage of the *Little Theatre,* after his long Indifpofition. Mr. Foote fuffer'd the removal of his Leg after a terrible Mifadventure, occafion'd by the rafh Japery of His Royal Highnefs, PRINCE EDWARD.

Prince Edward, Mr. Foote, & others were vifiting the EARL of MEXBOROUGH at *Cannons,* his Houfe in *Hampfhire,* in *February* of this Year. Mr. Foote not being thought of as a horfeman of the fineft Calibre, in fpite of that Gentleman's avowals to the contrary, His Highnefs fought to enjoy fome fport at his theatrickal Intimate's expenfe, & brought out an unbroken Mount upon which Mr. Foote might demonftrate his boafted equeftrian Proficiency.

No fooner had Mr. Foote fettl'd himfelf in his Saddle than the Horfe bolted, & its Rider was thrown with terrible Force to the ground. His Leg fuftain'd a grave Injury, & the Prince fent immediately to London for his royal Surgeon, upon whofe arrival an Amputation was perform'd, to curtail Putrefaction.

Mr. Foote has fhewn great Courage & Fortitude of late, tho' he has confided to his Friends that he has often been weak from Pain, enjoying no Sleep without recourfe to Opiates. His Highnefs is confum'd by Contrition, & has done all in his Power to enfure that his Friend's Profpects & Livelihood are not imping'd upon too adverfely by thefe unfortunate Circumftances. A royal Licence for his *Little Theatre* is lately granted, & Mr. Foote now makes ufe of a gold-topt Cane, & Two cork Legs, one of which is of a plain Defign, the other being array'd in a Silk-ftocking & a Court-fhoe with a filver Buckle.

Of TWO HIGHWAYMEN, meafur'd for their GRAVES.

30th of JULY – Two High-Tobymen of Nottinghamfhire, WILLIAM WAINER & JAMES BROMAGE, receiv'd Sentences of Death for the Plundering of a Coach on the KING's Highway. They were carry'd from the *Shire Hall* in *Nottingham* to *St. Mary's Church, High Pavement,* to hear the Execution Sermon. Thereafter, they were taken to their Graves in that Church-yard, & were made to lie in them for the purpofes of enfuring that the Excavations were of fufficient Size to accommodate their mortal Remains. They were later taken to the place of Execution, near *St. Andrew's Church,* where Sentence was carry'd out. Their Bodies were interr'd fome Hours afterwards in the Graves they had earlier vifited.

The SEVEN DIALS STROLLER

Remarks upon Mr. TENDUCCI, the *CASTRATO*, & his NEW BRIDE.

DAMNATION feize me if I do not have a round, *unvarnifh'd Tale* for the telling ! *Aficionados* of Mufick will be familiar with the celebrated *Sienefe Caftrato*, Mr. GIUSTO FERDINANDO TENDUCCI, and the fweet ftrains of his incomparable Voice, but I will lay you a Wager that they will be dumbfounded beyond all poffible Defcription by the hitherto unfeen Amoroufnefs in that Gentleman's Character, which has lately reveal'd itfelf to the World !

To the Aftonifhment of all, and the Rancour of fome, Mr. Tenducci was marry'd in *Cork, Ireland,* on the 19th Day of *Auguft,* to Mifs DOROTHEA MAUNSELL, the Daughter of Fifteen Years to Mr. THOMAS MAUNSELL, a Lawyer of *Dublin.* The Ceremony was perform'd by a Prieft of the *Catholick* Faith, and the *Caftrato's* Popery is the principal caufe of the *Animus* which now obtains between Mr. Tenducci and his choleric Father-in-Law. The *Proteftant* – and protefting – Mr. Maunfell feeks Redrefs, and has perfecuted the Couple with fuch relentlefs Determination that they have feen fit to elope.

O Ferdinando! I never knew you had the Balls to fee it through!

I can only poftulate that the Hufband's privy parts have not been deem'd deficient by the new Bride due only to her being entirely innocent in conjugal matters. I am, however, at a lofs to account for the manner in which fhe hopes to bear Progeny, which is – we are often told – the true Purpofe and defirable Confequence of Matrimony. The Method by which the Marriage has been or will be confummated muft alfo remain a matter of Conjecture.

The uxorious Mr. Tenducci has profecuted a chequer'd Career fince he firft arriv'd in *England* in 1758, and fome Years ago he languifh'd for a fpell of Eight Months in a Debtors' Prifon. His Fortunes foon enjoy'd a revival, however, and he became a frequent and popular Performer at *Ranelagh-gardens.* Perhaps his greateft Succefs to date has been his Appearance as *Arbaces* at *Covent-garden,* in Dr. ARNE's much-admir'd Opera, *Artaxerxes.* He fettl'd in *Dublin* in the Summer of laft Year, and fince then has enjoy'd the Plaudits of many Audiences in that fine City. For my part, befuddl'd tho' I am by his new domeftick Circumftances, I wifh him and his Wife every Happinefs that *Hymen* fees fit to beftow.

Of TISSOT's Treatife upon the DANGERS of MASTURBATION, lately publifh'd.

A Work entitl'd ONANISM ; or A Treatife Upon the Diforders produced by MASTURBATION, by the foreign Gentleman, SAMUEL AUGUSTE ANDRÉ DAVID TISSOT, is now publifh'd in Englifh, & feeks to warn its Readers of the dangerous Effects of fecret & exceffive Venery.

It is the Contention of the Author that Semen is an effential Oil, & a Stimulus, & its exceffive & habitual Difcharge from the Body precipitates all manner of Afflictions, amongft which are Gout, Rheumatifm, Blood in the Urine, weakening of the Organs of Generation, impair'd Vifion, lofs of Appetite, Head-aches, nervous Diforders, & the diminution of Strength, Reafon, & Memory. If thefe Affertions are to be believ'd, then this Nation is furely burden'd with the moft enfeebl'd coterie of Parliamentarians & Peers in Europe.

Particulars concerning Mr. GEORGE ALEXANDER STEVENS,
& his Satirickal *LECTURE Upon HEADS.*

FOR thefe Three Years paft, that *Choice Spirit*, Mr. STEVENS, has delighted the City & the Provinces with what he punningly calls a *Caput-all* Exhibition, being his fingular & original *LECTURE Upon HEADS*, which offers comickal & fatirickal Obfervations upon all the Ranks, Trades, & Claffes in the Nation.

Mr. Stevens now delights the good Citizens of *Stratford-Upon-Avon* with his Entertainment, which was firft given at the *Little Theatre* in the *Haymarket*, in *April* of the Year 1764, & has been widely enjoy'd in *London*, in many *Englifh* Towns & Cities, & in Dublin. To animate his Narration, he difplays a prodigious Number of Portrait Heads, render'd in Wood & *Papier Mâché*, the Apparel & Phyfiognomy of which are expreffive of thofe Characters & Occupations which he ridicules to great Mirth & Acclaim.

Amongft the Butts of his Mockery are pettifogging Lawyers, Quack Phyficians, Clergymen, Ladies of Fafhion, Amorous Fairs of the Town, *Billingfgate* Fifh-wives, Men of Learning, Artifts, Stockjobbers, & fundry Foreigners; all the Profeffions are *Caricatur'd* before the Publick with the utmoft Humour & Gaiety. Mr. Stevens knows well how to imitate their Voices, their Looks, & their Manner, & thofe delicate *Connoiffeurs* in Wit & Humour, having fuch weak Nerves that they are apt to faint away at the Sound of a Pun, are advif'd not to attend a Performance without Hartfhorn, *Eau de Luce*, or *Sal Volatile*.

This modifh Diverfion has brought Mr. Stevens his greateft Succefs to date, improving both his Circumftances, & his Reputation, which has hitherto been that of an incorrigible Libertine, & the maladroit Author of a Thoufand bawdy Songs & obfcene Treatifes. He was until the Year 1764 one of Mr. GARRICK's *Drury-lane* Company, & a fpirited Adherent of many intemperate Clubs in *London*. He is faid upon one Occafion to have thrown a Waiter out of a Window, & to have inftructed the Landlord of the Houfe to add the Lofs of the fellow to his Reckoning.

Of the ADULTEROUS ASSOCIATION of *LADY DI* & Mr. TOPHAM BEAUCLERK, lately culminating in WEDLOCK.

IT is now eſtabliſh'd that Mr. TOPHAM BEAUCLERK has crown'd with ultimate Poſſeſſion his longſtanding & ſcandalous Attachment to the accompliſh'd Artiſt, *Divorcée,* & Daughter of the DUKE of MARLBOROUGH, Lady BOLINGBROKE, marrying her as he did on the Twelfth of laſt Month.

While the ſottiſh Vifcount BOLINGBROKE ſuffer'd no Difficulties in breaking his victorious Horſe *GIMCRACK,* he did not enjoy ſimilar Succeſs in reining in his ſkittiſh Wife, whoſe *Amour* with Mr. Beauclerk has reſulted in the Birth of Two Children, & the late Bill for the Diſſolution of the Marriage, which was paſſ'd by royal Aſſent on the 10th of *March.* We have learn'd that Depofitions at Readings of the Bill, by a Footman of Lady Bolingbroke's Reſidence in *Mayfair,* atteſt to the incontrovertible Proofs of the Pair's laſcivious Embraces on a *Sofa,* & to the clandeſtine Attendance of Two Phyſicians upon her Ladyſhip during the Birth of Mr. Beauclerk's baſtard Child.

Her Ladyſhip was born Lady DIANA SPENCER, & her youthful Aptitude for Drawing flouriſh'd

There are Three-hundred of us in this Marriage...

Mr. BEAUCLERK & Lady DI

under the Tutelage of the eſteem'd Artiſt, Mr. JOSHUA REYNOLDS. She was join'd in Matrimony to Viſcount Bolingbroke in *September* of the Year 1757, tho' Rumours of his Lordſhip's Debauchery having unhappy Effects upon the Marriage abounded from its earlieſt Days. She is known to her intimate Circle as *LADY DI.*

Mr. Beauclerk is the Great-grandſon of the late KING CHARLES the SECOND & his Paramour NELL GWYN, & he is ſaid to reſemble that Monarch markedly. He is infamous for the laxity of his Habits, being filthy in his Perſon, & allowing a prodigious Quantity of Vermin to thrive in his Perruque. It is noted by many that he frequently leaves behind him Infeſtations of Lice, that plague the Houſeholds he has viſited, & his new Bride is oblig'd to change daily the Linen of the marital Bed. He is allow'd to be a Gentleman of Wit & Learning, & is a favour'd Intimate of Dr. SAMUEL JOHNSON, tho' there exiſts between theſe two Friends a tacit Accord that Mr. Beauclerk ſhould never offend the Ears & Senſibilities of the great Johnſon with boaſts or anecdotes of his Infidelities & Licentiouſneſs.

An ACCOUNT of the AMPUTATION
of Mr. JOSIAH WEDGWOOD's LEG.

THAT moſt enterpriſing of Tradeſmen, Mr. JOSIAH WEDGWOOD, has lately ſuffer'd his Leg to be taken off above his Knee, & has aſtounded his Friends with the uncomplaining Manner in which he has endur'd the loſs.

Mr. Wedgwood was unfortunate in contracting the Small-pox in his youth, during the Outbreak of that fearſome Malady, that afflicted the People of *Staffordſhire* many Years hence. He was render'd lame in his right Leg, & this prov'd ſomething of a Hindrance in his choſen Trade, ſince he is unable to uſe the Kick-wheel for the throwing of Pots. The Impairment led him undaunted towards Experimentation in the Materials & Fabrication of Pottery, & he has eſtabliſh'd a moſt induſtrious Manufactory known as ETRURIA, near *Newcaſtle-under-Lyme*, & a faſhionable metropolitan Ware-houſe on *Charles-ſtreet*, near *Groſvenor-ſquare*. Her Majeſty Queen CHARLOTTE is become his moſt honour'd Patron.

In recent Months, Mr. Wedgwood found the Pain that his weaken'd Limb occaſion'd him to be intolerable, & it was concluded that an Amputation had become the only certain Remedy. Mr. Wedgwood's Friend, Dr. ERASMUS DARWIN, ſent for the Surgeon, Mr. JAMES BENT, who perform'd the Taſk on the 31st Day of *May*. Mr. THOMAS BENTLEY & Mr. Wedgwood's WIFE alſo attended the Proceedings, during which the Gentleman was ſeated upright in his Chair, having beforehand taken a draught of *Laudanum*, which did not dull his Wits to the extent that he was unable to obſerve the buſineſs in its Entirety, which was his wiſh. A *Tourniquet* was faſten'd about the Thigh, the fleſh was cut, & the Bone was ſawn through with great Swiftneſs & Dexterity. The Bandages have lately come off, & Mr. Wedgwood's Reſtoration to full Health & Mobility, with the aſſiſtance of a wooden Leg, now ſeems aſſur'd.

The SEVEN DIALS STROLLER

A SCANDALOUS REVELATION concerning
the late Mr. SAMUEL DERRICK, the *LITTLE KING of BATH.*

MY devoted Readers will corroborate the Affertion that I rarely fpeak ill of the Deceaf'd, but a long-held Secret of *fuch delicious Novelty* has late reach'd my Ears that it would be remifs of me to keep it for myfelf, for fear of tarnifhing a dead Man's already queftionable Reputation.

It is let flip that the *Mafter of Ceremonies* at *Bath*, Mr. SAMUEL DERRICK, was the true and fole Author of the PIMP-GENERAL HARRIS's *LIST of COVENT-GARDEN LADIES*, even until the very Day of his Paffing, being the 28th of *March*! What is more, I have learn'd that, by his Will, the Revenue accru'd by the lateft Edition of this infamous Work fhall go to his Friend, the fhamelefs *Cyprian &* Bawd, Mrs. CHARLOTTE HAYES. Mr. Derrick fettl'd upon his Whoremonger's *Kalendar* as a method of reviving his Fortunes, after his literary Purfuits founder'd, and Debauchery ravag'd his Purfe. He ftruck a Bargain with Jack Harris, entailing the Publication *&* Embellifhment of that Pimp's Lift of Harlots, and pecuniary Rewards fwiftly follow'd.

It is laughable, is it not, that a man who fought to prefent to the World a Character of Refpectability and Rank, and who hop'd to efcape the Bonds of his humble beginnings as a *Dublin* Linen-draper, and an inferior Poet, fhould have feen fit to fund his Afcent through polite Circles by fuch bafe means ?

It may be faid of Mr. Derrick that Opinions of him are, at beft, ambivalent. It was not without confiderable Oppofition in *Bath* that he was elected to the Pofition of *Mafter of Ceremonies*. Compar'd with his great Predeceffor, Mr. Beau NASH, he was confider'd *fo fmall and pufillanimous in his Appearance, that it was next to impoffible for him to command Refpect.* Dr. SAMUEL JOHNSON confefs'd to a liking for the Fellow, yet even he, when afk'd if he thought Derrick or Mr. CHRISTOPHER SMART the better Poet, lamented that there was *no fettling the point of Precedency between a Loufe and a Flea.* Mr. JAMES BOSWELL once entertain'd hopes that Derrick would prefent him to Dr. Johnfon, but no Introduction ever tranfpir'd, leaving Mr. Boswell with the Sufpicion that he had promif'd *to do what was not in his Power.* He fhew'd the rakifh *Scotchman* Bofwell *the fhabbier afpects of London, in all its Variety of departments, both literary and fportive,* for which one might fuppofe Bofwell fhould have felt indebted to Derrick, yet he ftill confider'd the Fellow *a little blackguard pimping Dog.*

Forgive, we befeech Thee O Lord,
The Soul of SAM DERRICK the Bawd,
Since Fortune has kifs'd
Whores defcrib'd in his LIST,
And the Price of their Favours has foar'd

R.I.P.

Of the CREMATION of Mrs. HONORETTA PRATT,
being the FIRST in our NATION.

Mrs. Pratt believ'd that the Vapours, or *Miasma*, arising from Graves in the Church-yards of populous Cities, must prove hurtful to their Inhabitants. She resolv'd to extend to the Living of present & future Times – as far as it was within her Power – that Charitable Benevolence which is affirm'd by her Friends & Relations to have distinguish'd her Character throughout her Life. This venerable Lady was born in the Time of King CHARLES SECOND, & was a Correspondent of the late Dr. JONATHAN SWIFT. It is the Opinion of the Publishers of this News-sheet that a Woman who has known so much of Life & its Vicissitudes should have the Honour of chusing the Circumstances of her own Obsequies.

26th SEPTEMBER ——

Mrs. HONORETTA PRATT, the Widow of Mr. JOHN PRATT, & the Daughter of Sir JOHN BROOKES of *York,* was burnt in an open Grave at *St. George's Burial-ground, Hanover-square, Middlesex,* on the Day immediately following her Death. This was perform'd upon the Place where her dear late Niece, ANN PLACE, lies bury'd, in accordance with Mrs. Pratt's Wishes. Her Cremation is the First your Editor has heard of in this City, or indeed in this Nation.

She order'd that her Body should be burnt in the Hope that others would follow her Example, which is now too hastily censur'd by those who have not enquir'd the Motive. The Lawfulness of the Cremation has elicited much Debate, as has the precise nature of its Execution, since it is thought by many that unslak'd lime was us'd to consume the Body by chymickal means, in place of Fire.

I should prefer mine a trifle underdone...

PART the THIRD
1770-1779

It is an ineluctable fact of Life that no Man can have all things go his own way indefinitely, & I must own that the Eighth Decade of our Century was not entirely kind to the Editor of this modest Compendium. When the Fates take against a fellow, his natural stock of Chearfulness is bound to be depleted as a Consequence.

In the Year 1771, I began to cultivate hopes of Matrimony, which had thus far eluded me in the manner of a greas'd Weasel. The Object of my Affection was a sweet-natur'd Governess & Daughter of a *White-Chapel* Apothecary, but her confounded Father would not consent to the Match, citing the Wound I receiv'd aboard Ship as a certain hindrance to the begetting of Heirs. In a shameful funk, I broke with my *Inamorata*, resign'd myself to a Life devoid of connubial Bliss, & vow'd to trouble the Fairer Sex no more. Hard work, I soon found, is physick for the Heart & Mind.

Until the Year 1775, my beloved *Gazette* enjoy'd the Benefits of robust & not wholly dishonourable Rivalry from other Periodickals, which enabl'd me to keep my wits sharp & my Ambition in rude Health. Yet the appointment of the *Reverend HENRY BATE* to the position of Editor at the *Morning Post* soon shook many a News-sheet Proprietor out of his Complacency. This canting SCOUNDREL & RUFFIAN was notorious in polite Society as an impetuous Duellist & Pugilist, who would call out enemies & gainsayers on the slightest Pretext. I confess to a sneaking admiration for the rascal's Tenacity & Cunning in the sniffing out of Scandal for the pages of his Publication, yet I cannot feel aught but an implacable Resentment for the manner in which he set about trampling upon his Peers & Rivals. As a Consequence of Bate's *Stratagems*, I was forc'd to double the size of the financial Inducements I gave to the servants & Householders of the Nobility, for the Intelligence they supply'd concerning the Eccentricities & Peccadilloes of their Employers. I also felt oblig'd to offer increas'd remuneration to the *Seven-Dials Stroller*, lest he be entic'd away from my *Gazette* by the ample Purse of the blackguard Bate.

Mr. Jakes continu'd a plaguesome Dog, who now number'd gaming amongst his degenerate Diversions, & he attended the Cock-fights in *Westminster* whenever the Humour took him. The outcome of a match in *December* 1778 was most hotly & violently disputed by the Spectators, & Jakes lost an Eye in grappling with a pugnacious Swine-gelder. My own medickal abilities being unequal to the Task, & the Pox having carry'd Dr. Shinsaw to the Almighty the previous Year, I dipp'd in to my ravag'd Capital to procure the foolish jackanapes chirurgical Assistance. I am happy to record that his artistick Faculties were not hamper'd by this barbarous usage.

The Year 1770 saw the proud *Coquette* & infamous Hostess *Mrs. CORNELYS* at the *Zenith* of her Powers. Her lavish *Masquerades* & Assemblies at *Carlisle House* sent a thrill of INTRIGUE through the Fashionable World. ———

The Gin-Lane Gazette

PUBLISHED in LONDON   *March, 1770.*   Nathaniel Crowquill Efq.

Particulars concerning Mrs. TERESA CORNELYS, & her SCANDALOUS *MASQUERADES* at *Carliſle Houſe.*

By N. CROWQUILL, *Editor.*

THE *Beau Monde* efteem nothing more highly than Novelty, & that *High Prieſteſs* of faſhionable Entertainments, Mrs. CORNELYS, is pleaſ'd to fupply her Patrons at *Carliſle Houſe* with every wondrous & extravagant Innovation that they could ever crave, perfecting as ſhe has the Art of the *Maſquerade* above any Example yet feen in *London.* Mrs. Cornelys took the Leaſe of her Houſe in *Soho-Square* in the Year 1761, & has improv'd it beyond all poſſible Defcription, with the addition of a commodious & beguiling Aſſembly Room ; a *Chineſe* Bridge, believ'd to have been built to a Defign by Mr. Thos. CHIPPENDALE ; Looking-glaſſes & curious *Chineſe* Plaſterwork upon the Walls ; an Apfe fet about with Columns, wherein her Muficians perform ; & countlefs Chandeliers, accommodating Four-thoufand Candles to illuminate the Revels of her Patrons.

Each Year, ſhe gives Twelve Balls & Twelve Suppers to the Nobility, & an equal Number to the Middling Sort, & boafts that ſhe has, upon many Occafions, entertain'd Six-hundred Guefts at Two *Guineas* a Head. We are given to underftand ſhe is in receipt of £24,000 *per annum,* which cannot be wonder'd at, fince it often feems that the whole World flocks to her Eftablifhment in a fingle Evening, & her Rooms are frequently fo hot & fo crowded that Dancing is not even attempted. The Carriages of the Nobility, thronging to her door, fuffer Collifions & Damage with

fuch regularity that Mrs. Cornelys is now oblig'd to infift in her Advertifements that Coachmen muft all procefs to & from her Premifes in one Direction only, with the Horfes' heads pointed towards *Greek-ſtreet.*

It is faid that Mrs. Cornelys has expended a confiderable part of her Revenue in eftablifhing a paftoral retreat in *Hammerſmith,* where ſhe keeps Thirty-two Servants, Three Secretaries, Six Horfes, a Mute, a boon Companion of her own Sex, & a Child father'd by *Signor* CASANOVA, her former *Beau.*

Yet for all that the Quality is undoubtedly enchanted by the Allurements of *Carliſle Houſe,* Mrs. Cornelys & her Enterprife are not without Detractors. Laft Month, *Parliament* was adjourn'd prematurely, to allow Members to attend one of her *Maſquerades,* which might be deem'd a fcandalous Dereliction of publick Duty.

Her moft recent Ball was attended by one Captain WATSON, a Guards Officer, who appear'd as a naked ADAM, wearing clofe-fitting Silk the colour of Flefh, upon which were embroider'd Fig-leaves that adher'd fo tightly to the privy parts underneath that the indelicate Effect produc'd was remark'd upon by all prefent. It is alfo hotly difputed whether the very Anonymity & Concealment that the *Maſquerade* demands, & the Familiarity & Intercourfe between Ranks both high & low that are fuch an undifcriminating Entertainment's inevitable concomitant, are in any wife to be defir'd or encourag'd.

Price : Fourpence.

Of Mr. JOHN HUNTER, & his EXOTICK ANIMALS at *Earl's Court.*

THE good Burghers of *Earl's Court* may be forgiven for fuppofing that a latter-day *Eden* is fprung up in their midft, fince the Anatomift Mr. JOHN HUNTER eftablifh'd in that Parifh a *Menagerie* of fundry exotick Beafts, with which he appears to commune, in a kind of prelapfarian Ataraxy.

On an Eftate of Two Acres, Mr. Hunter keeps Buffaloes, Goats, Stallions, & Sheep in his Stables, & Leopards & Jackals in a Den. There are alfo Oftriches, & Serpents, Silk-worms feafting upon a Mulberry-tree, Hives for Bees, & a Pond accommodating Ducks & Geefe.

Yet Mr. Hunter fhews himfelf aptly nam'd, & proves more of a NIMROD than an ADAM, fince he keeps thefe Creatures only that he & his Circle of young Followers might flaughter, diffect & anatomife many of them to advance the Caufe of *Natural Philofophy.* He has made Experiments & Obfervations upon the Air-facs of Eagles, the Gizzards of Owls, Hawks, & Gulls, the Spurs of Fowls, & the Bones of Pigs. He has alfo inveftigated divers Curiofities of Nature, fuch as the methods by which Lizards generate heat in their Bodies, & has made clofe Studies of Dormice, Wolves, Opoffums, prickly Hedgehogs, the Moaning of Dingoes, & the Barking of Beagles. If his Difciples' thirft for Knowledge demands it, he has been known to augment his ftock of *Specimens* with the Carcaffes of deceaf'd Exhibits from the Royal Menagerie at the *Tower of London.*

The 15th of this MONTH - The Lawyer & Antiquary, Mr. DAINES BARRINGTON, prefented to the *Royal Society* his **ACCOUNT of a VERY REMARKABLE YOUNG MUSICIAN,** in which he defcrib'd & affirm'd the Genius of the Boy **WOLFGANG MOZART,** as witnefs'd by him during the Child's Vifit to London in the Year 1764.

Mr. Barrington recounts how he fet before Mafter Mozart a Duet unknown to him, & how the Boy unhefitatingly took the *Soprano* part, allotted the *Alto* part to his Father, & play'd the figur'd *Bafs,* while interpofing when neceffary the Violin parts. Such an Ability requires the fimultaneous reading of many different *Clefs,* & Mr. Barrington made plain the Difficulty of the Feat by likening it to reading fimultaneoufly divers paffages of Poefy, each of which has its own modes of Expreffion, Character, & rhetorickal Rules, & each of which is written in *Greek, Hebrew,* & *Arabick* Characters. Mr. Barrington entreated the *Royal Society* to efteem Mafter Mozart's Performance as akin to a capital Speech in Shakefpeare never feen before, & yet read by a Child of Eight Years old, with all the pathetick Energy of a GARRICK.

BUGGS,

BE they ever fo numerous, are effectually deftroy'd out of Bedheads, Furniture, Walls, Paper, &c. by ANDREW COOKE, at the *King's Arms, Holborn-Hill.* A Line directed to my Houfe, No.6, in *Union-Court,* where I have liv'd near 30 Years, will be duly anfwer'd, & will prevent many Difputes with Vagrants that lurk about my Houfe, in Order to intercept my Cuftomers & direct them elfewhere. Some Rivals report that I am Dead, in order to obtain my Bufinefs. I am a Tall Thin Man, & always in the Bufinefs myfelf, being known in Town & Country to have clear'd by Yearly Contract upwards of 10,000 Beds, to great Applaufe, the Buggs not returning for a Number of Years, & the Beds ready for immediate Ufe if requir'd, without the leaft Stain or Damage — 1s. 6d.

My Abilities in this Profeffion are attefted to at the *London-Tavern, Bifhopfgate-Street* ; the Afylum, Weftminfter-Bridge ; the *Foundling Hofpital* ; 10 Boarding Schools ; Bankers' Offices ; & a Number of Coffee-houfes, & Lodging-houfes, not chufing to have their Names mention'd.

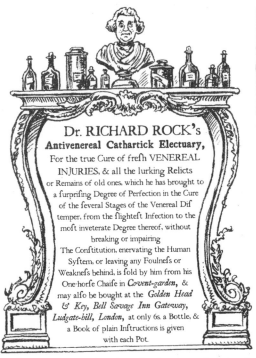

The **28th of August** - IT was thought politick to defer a Benefit Performance at the *Canterbury Theatre* by the Actress, Mrs. DYER, in favour of a much-anticipated CRICKET MATCH, held before a large Company of genteel Spectators at *Bourne Place*, Half-way between *Canterbury & Dover*. *Middlesex & Surrey* prevail'd against Bourne, at the Ground establish'd there by Sir HORACE MANN, upon the Paddock before his Mansion.

The SEVEN DIALS STROLLER

An Account of Mr. GEORGE HANGER's Abandonment by his GYPSY WIFE.

I am not in the Business of preaching at my Readers, but the matrimonial Misadventure suffer'd of late by Mr. GEORGE HANGER must serve as a cautionary Parable for any young Gentleman seeking to hitch his connubial Cart to the alluring but fickle Charms of wayfaring Maidens.

Mr. Hanger is in the first bloom of Manhood, being but Twenty Years of Age, and has purchas'd for himself an Ensigncy in the *1st Regiment of Foot-guards*. Perhaps the swaggering Self-possession that Youth and a new-found Position in the World can engender have misled the Fellow into supposing that he is unconquerable in all things, not least Affairs of the Heart. When station'd to the South of *London*, he fell into company with a musickal Gypsy-girl, who play'd a *Dulcimer* beyond all comparison, and to whose sweet, melodick Voice he would listen in Transports of Rapture. The dark Beauty became known to Hanger and his martial Confederates as the *lovely Aegypta of Norwood*, and with unseemly haste he made her his Wife !

I am sorry to relate that this conjugal Gladness has prov'd a Delusion, as his Aegypta has of late elop'd with a spindle-legg'd Tinker, who roams the Country plying his Trade as a Mender of Pots, and Kettles. To be cast aside so carelessly in favour of such a low-born Vagrant will be keenly felt by Mr. Hanger as a Wound to his Honour, but I am able to foresee, with Gypsy Prescience, that the swiving Spirit will soon course vigorously again through his Veins, and, *Lethe*-like, expunge this unhappy Attachment from his Remembrance.

But I spent a Twelvemonth's Allowance on my big, fat Gypsy Wedding!

The Gin-Lane Gazette

PUBLISHED in LONDON   *October, 1771.*   Nathaniel Crowquill Efq.

Particulars Concerning the VIOLENT REBELLION by the BOYS of HARROW SCHOOL againſt their MASTERS.

WHINING School-boys might creep like Snails unwillingly to School, yet they will gladly ruſh headlong towards Brickbats & MUTINY, if the late Actions of the Striplings at HARROW SCHOOL offer creditable Indications as to the true nature of YOUTH.

The Death of Mr. SUMNER having neceſſitated the Appointment of a new Head-maſter by the Governors of that School, the young Maſter, Mr. SAMUEL PARR, faw fit to advance his own Candidature, feeking the Patronage of Lord DARTMOUTH in this Endeavour, & afferting that his boyhood Attendance at *Harrow*, & his being a local Man, muſt render him an unparallel'd Applicant. Two Maſters of ETON SCHOOL, namely Mr. BENJAMIN HEATH, & the late Head-maſter's Couſin, Mr. HUMPHREY SUMNER, also announc'd their intereſt in the Poſition, & much robuſt lobbying by all Parties enſu'd.

After fome curfory Deliberations, the Governors elected unanimouſly the Etonian Mr. Heath as Head-maſter on the 3rd of *October*, & gave the fuccefsful Candidate a Dinner, to which the aggriev'd Mr. Parr was not invited. Parr confronted the Gentlemen, damning them for their *Meanneſs, Injuſtice, & Perfidy*, but was infom'd that his being but Four-and-Twenty Years of Age was the principal Barrier to his Preferment. A Throng of *Harrow*'s Boys – who favour'd & eſteem'd Mr. Parr greatly as a Maſter & an Old *Harrovian* – were gather'd in the vicinity, & air'd their Fury at Mr. Heath's Appointment most vehemently, demanding to know whether it was fit that they ſhould *always take up with the Refuſe of ETON*. A Petition was got up by Three Members of the Fifth Form, to which

Twenty-fix of the Boys put their Names, before prefenting it to the Governors. *Harrow*, in their Opinion, *ought not to be conſider'd as an Appendix to Eton*, & this was their Petition's chief Afſertion.

The Governors were affronted by this faucy Undertaking, & one of their number condemn'd the Petitioners as *no better than a Parcel of Blackguards*. In Retaliation, the Boys fet about fmaſhing his Carriage, took away its Wheels, & fet it tumbling down *Sudbury-hill*. Not content with this, they broke the Windows of both the School-houfe, & another Governor's Refidence, & chalk'd the Motto *PARR FOR EVER* upon the Carriages of others. Riot, Rebellion, & rough Ufage continu'd for fome confiderable time, & Mr. Heath made good his Efcape, fcurrying back to *Eton*.

Mr. Parr did all in his Power to fubdue the turbulent Malcontents, & their Proteſtations had no laſting effect upon the Refolution of the Governors to fee Mr. Heath inftall'd as Head-maſter. Order has now been impoſ'd upon *Harrow*, but at fome confiderable coſt, fince Fifty Boys have elected to quit the School with the Acquiefcence of their Parents. We underſtand that Mr. Parr intends to eſtabliſh his own School at *Stanmore-hill*, but the Wifdom of allowing any Child to come under the Tutelage of a Man who is an avow'd Supporter of the infamous Radickal, Libertine, & Perpetrator of Baboon Japery, Mr. JOHN WILKES, muſt certainly be deem'd queſtionable.

Price : Fourpence.

The SEVEN DIALS STROLLER

Of the PROFLIGATE GAMING of Mr. CHARLES JAMES FOX ; A WAYWARD SON to a FOND FATHER.

THE indulgence of a doting Parent will more often than not lead to the Ruination of the Child, and HENRY FOX, Lord HOLLAND, could certainly have such an Accusation lay'd to his Charge. His Son, *The Hon.* Mr. CHARLES JAMES FOX M.P., proves himself by turns an inveterate Gamester, as the Intelligence I have to relate will testify.

Not content with purchasing for his Son in 1768 the Constituency of *Midhurst*, in *Sussex* – tho' the Youth was but Nineteen Years old, hence, on a point of Technicality, ineligible for Parliament – His Lordship has of late settl'd Charles's gaming Debts, and it has cost him the pretty sum of £20,000 to do so. The necessity of this Expedient cannot surprise young Fox's Intimates when they consider how his love of Play governs his mode of Life.

On Tuesday, the Fourth Day of this Month, Fox sat up playing *Hazard* at *Almack's Assembly Rooms*, until Five O'Clock in the Afternoon of the following Day, during which time he lost £12,000, recover'd the same sum, and ended by losing £11,000. On the Thursday, he spoke feebly at a Debate in the *House of Commons*, din'd after Eleven O'Clock that Evening, and afterwards repair'd to *White's Club*, where he drank Heroically until

Damn me, Madam! Will you not afford me the least Satisfaction?!

The MACARONI SUITOR,
Or,—Mr. CHARLES JAMES Fox propositions DAME FORTUNE.

Seven in the Morning. Returning to Almack's, he won £6,000, before striking out for *Newmarket* to lay Wagers on his beloved Nags. His Brother, Mr. STEPHEN FOX, lost £11,000 Two Nights after the abovemention'd Forays, and Charles bade farewell to a further £10,000 on the 13th of *February*, which, by my Calculations, means that in Three Nights, the Two Siblings piss'd away £32,000 between them !

I have witness'd Fox and his Circle at play, and singularly amusing it is to see them set such store by the curious Talismans they employ as Propitiations to fickle *Dame Fortuna*. They pull off the habitual, embroider'd garb of the fashionable *Macaroni*, and either don Greatcoats, or turn their Coats inside outwards for good luck. They wear straw Hats with broad Rims and high Crowns, bedeckt with

Ribbons and Flowers, to shield their Eyes from the Light, and to keep in place their red or blue powder'd Hair. To spare their lace Ruffles they put on leather guards, such as those worn by Footmen when they polish Cutlery.

Stricter paternal Governance and Censure in his formative Years would surely have nipped Charles's Prodigality in the Bud, but Lord Holland's Indulgence of his Son in his Boyhood knew no bounds. Upon one Occasion, he did nothing when Charles smash'd his Watch before his Eyes. Upon another, His Lordship forgot his Promise to Charles that he might witness the Demolition of a Wall, and, to rectify this Oversight, had it built up again before knocking it down in the Child's Presence. In his Youth, Lord Holland sent Charles to *France,* where he might exercise his burgeoning *Libido,* and he took up with a Silversmith's Wife at Nice, boasting to a Friend that *I was a long time here before I could get a Fuck, but in recompense for my Sufferings, I have got a more excellent Piece that must be allowed.* Nowadays, he readily confesses to his close Circle that *fucking* in *Cundums* and *Frigging* are his chief Employments in Town. At his Birth, Lord Holland remark'd of the swarthy and hirsute Charles that he resembl'd nothing less than a MONKEY, and in his love of Mischief, Play, and Frivolities, the Boy has shewn his Father's Appraisal of him to have been imbu'd with startling Prescience.

The Gin-Lane Gazette

PUBLISHED in LONDON   *June, 1772.*   Nathaniel Crowquill Efq.

Of the CALAMITY in BANKING, & the Meafures taken by the BANK of ENGLAND to bolfter our Nation's FISCAL INTERESTS.

THE Preponderance of our Readers will by now be aware of the fingular & troubling Threat pof'd to our entire Syftem of Banking, which was brought about by the fecklefs Stockjobbing of Mr. ALEXANDER FORDYCE. The Collapfe of the financial Houfe of Meffrs. NEALE, JAMES, DOWN, & FORDYCE, on the Day lately dubb'd *Black Monday,* has led to the Failure of almoft every private Bank in *Scotland,* & to fifcal Difafters in *London, Edinburgh,* & *Amfterdam.*

Fordyce had been engag'd in recklefs Speculation, fhorting Stock to a prodigious Degree in the EAST INDIA COMPANY, & appropriating the Depofits of his Houfe's Patrons to cover his Loffes. The fifcal Plight this has precipitated is thought to be the moft difaftrous fince the Infamy of the *South-Sea Bubble* of fome Fifty-two Years hence ; the BANK of ENGLAND fhall be forc'd to intercede, & to affift thofe Financial Houfes at moft rifk. Fordyce's Partners aforemention'd are declar'd Bankrupt, & the Scoundrel himfelf fled *London* for *France* on the 10th Day of *June.* On the Eve of his Departure, Fordyce is faid to have return'd to his Home in ungovernable Spirits, & to have declar'd the following to his Houfehold :- *I always told the wary Ones & the wife Ones that I would be a Man*

MILKING the DRY DAME,
or, — The Old Lady of Threadneedle-ftreet fuckling her Fat Cat.

or a Moufe ; & this Night, this very Night, the Die is caft, & I am A MAN! Bring Champagne ! And Butler, Burgundy below ! Let Tonight live for ever ! ALEXANDER IS A MAN !

Trade in our Nation is greatly hinder'd by thefe Events, & the financial Stabilitie of *North Britain* is perilous undermin'd. The continuance of moft Publick Amufements & theatrickal Performances is lately difcontinu'd, or in doubt. Many Actors of note had feen fit to inveft their Fortunes in the bankrupt Houfe, & it is difficult to fee how their Circumftances might be reliev'd to any Degree, without the Expedient of Benefit Performances. Mr. JOHN ADAM, who is engag'd in Partnerfhip with his Brothers in the building of the much-anticipated *Adelphi* Edifices, is forc'd to difcharge Two-thoufand Labourers in his Employ, *pro tempore.*

Twenty-five Banks in *England* & *Scotland* are now thought to have fuffer'd irrevocable Failure, fince Fordyce fcurry'd difhonourably away from the fcene of his execrable Swindling.

Price : Fourpence.

Of Mrs. TERESA CORNELYS, & the Magnitude of her DEBTS.

The Circumſtances of Mrs. CORNELYS are degraded to ſuch a Degree that ſhe faces the Threat of PENURY. On the 22nd Day of this Month, *Carliſle Houſe*, its Chattels, & Furniſhings were ſold by Auction for the Sum of £.10,200 to a Company of her Creditors, amongſt whom was Mr. THOMAS CHIPPENDALE.

Mrs. Cornelys's Star began to wane laſt Year, when ſhe found herſelf under Indictment for the keeping of a Diforderly Houſe, wherein looſe, idle & riotous Men & Women in Maſques carouſ'd & miſbehav'd into the ſmall Hours of the Morning. Upon one Occaſion, a Guard of Thirty of the King's Men ejected licentious Revellers from the Houſe at Seven O'Clock in the *ante meridiem*, & Wine & Victuals were thrown from the Windows to the raucous Mob below. Mrs. Cornelys was alſo twice fin'd for preſenting Operas to her Patrons without a Royal Licenſe, after an Action inſtigated by certain enrag'd & jealous Theatrickal Managers. Her Plea of Mitigation that theſe Performances were Charitable Benefits, or merely *harmonic Meetings*, was difmiſſ'd by the Magiſtrates of *Bow-ſtreet*. Mrs. Cornelys's Daughter has now abandon'd her to her Fate.

Particulars concerning Mr. JAMES COX's remarkable MUSEUM of MECHANICKAL CURIOSITIES.

YOUR *Gazetteers* do not feel able to permit the Year to draw to its End without remarking upon Mr. COX's MUSEUM at the Great-room in *Spring-gardens, Charing-croſs*, which has delighted the *Bon Ton* throughout the Seaſon, & is allow'd by all to be a Houſe of extravagant, Clock-work WONDERS.

Contain'd therein – amongſt ſundry other Delights – are a Swan *Automaton*, that appears to ſwim upon moving Waters, preen its Plumage, catch a Fiſh, & ſwallow the ſame, to the Accompaniment of beguiling Muſick ; a Copper Statue of a Boy wearing a Hat, in which are conceal'd both muſickal Chimes, & a Pineapple that opens to diſcover a Neſt of Birds being fed precious Pearls by their Parent, fluttering about them ; an *Aſiatick* Temple of bejewell'd gold, ſet about with Palm-trees, Coral, & Crockodiles, & crown'd with a Dome, from which a *Pagoda* riſes to the Muſick of Chimes ; a ſizeable & ornamented Peacock Clock ; & an Elephant, ſtanding Nine Feet in Height.

Dr. SAMUEL JOHNSON, & his Acolyte, Mr. JAMES BOSWELL, are but Two of the Viſitors of ſtanding who have grac'd the Muſeum with their Patronage, & Mr. Cox has engag'd proper Perſons to explain to both Foreigners & Natives what each Piece performs in relation to its Muſick & Mechaniſm.

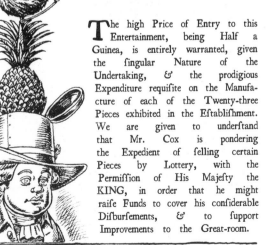

The high Price of Entry to this Entertainment, being Half a Guinea, is entirely warranted, given the ſingular Nature of the Undertaking, & the prodigious Expenditure requiſite on the Manufacture of each of the Twenty-three Pieces exhibited in the Eſtabliſhment. We are given to underſtand that Mr. Cox is pondering the Expedient of ſelling certain Pieces by Lottery, with the Permiſſion of His Majeſty the KING, in order that he might raiſe Funds to cover his conſiderable Diſburſements, & to ſupport Improvements to the Great-room.

VOTARY *of* Venus

We prefent to our Readers our Bold *Cyprian* for the Month of *May,*

MRS. SOPHIA BADDELEY.

THO' fhe is an indifferent Actrefs, defcrib'd by Mr. GARRICK as *an infpir'd Idiot* of the Stage, Mrs. BADDELEY is allow'd by her Admirers to have a tolerable finging Voice, & was taught Mufick by her Father, Mr. VALENTINE SNOW, who was Sergeant-Trumpeter to KING GEORGE the SECOND, & for whom the late Mr. HANDEL penn'd *Virtuofo* parts.

Mrs. Baddeley fings very often at *Ranelagh* & *Vauxhall,* & made the Song entitl'd *Sweet Willy O!* her own during Mr. Garrick's Shakefpeare *Jubilee* at *Stratford-upon-Avon.*

More than for any Theatrickal or Mufickal Accomplifhments, however, Mrs. Baddeley is admir'd for her fingular Beauty, which once fo enraptur'd the Violinift Dr. HERSCHEL, when fhe ftepp'd upon the Stage at Bath, that he dropt his Bow in Aftonifhment. Mr. JAMES BOSWELL has alfo praif'd her Charms as a *beautiful, infinuating Creature.*

Mrs. Baddeley was marry'd to the Actor Mr. ROBERT BADDELEY in the Year 1764, but fhe took up with a number of generous *Paramours,* perhaps with the Approval of her venal Hufband, & we underftand he once fought a Duel, not in defence of her Honour, but in difpute of her Salary. The Marriage being fince diffolv'd, fhe has been in High-keeping with feveral money'd Protectors, amongft whom are Vifcounts & Captains.

Gentlemen Admirers feeking to court this amorous Fair fhould be caution'd that fhe fets great Store by the Trinkets & Trappings of Luxury, & has accumulated a bewildering Quantity of Debts all over Town. She has quit the *Drury-lane Theatre* over a Quarrel with Mr. Garrick concerning her Salary, & fhe was lately wrefted from the clutches of a Creditor by her Friend, Mrs. ELIZA STEELE, who wore a Man's Cloaths to expedite the Refcue.

May 7th - WHILE the *Beau Monde* looks upon the Marriage of Mr. TOPHAM BEAUCLERK & *LADY DI* – the former Lady BOLINGBROKE – with a Degree of Leniency, it feems that Mr. JAMES BOSWELL has much left to do in refpect of perfuading Dr. SAMUEL JOHNSON that the Lady is of good Character.

While breakfafting at Mr. THRALE's, Mr. Bofwell held forth upon how *Lady Di* had been brutally ill-uf'd by her former Hufband, & that Mr. Beauclerk had won her Heart while fhe was thus unhappily fituated, & in the Prime of her Life. Mr. Bofwell's Efforts to palliate the adulterous Actions of Mr. & Mrs. Beauclerk notwithftanding, Dr. Johnfon check'd his Friend's Extenuation with the following Reproach : *My dear Sir, never accuftom your Mind to mingle Virtue & Vice. The Woman's a WHORE, & there's an end on't.*

Look for 'WHORE' in my DICTIONARY, & you fhall find the Lady's Picture, Sir!

Of the RITES of VENUS, perform'd at Mrs. CHARLOTTE HAYES's lewd *FEAST of OTAHEITE,* & attended by Gentlemen of the Firſt Rank.

THE celebrated Travels of *Captain* JAMES COOK amongſt the amorous Peoples of the *South Seas,* which are lately publiſh'd in Volumes edited by Mr. JOHN HAWKESWORTH, have entranc'd & titillated the Publick to ſuch a degree that Mrs. **CHARLOTTE HAYES** has lately ſeen fit to offer her Patrons a ſcandalous Performance of OTAHEITIAN VENERY.

Mrs. Hayes let it be known that her Eſtabliſhment in *King's-place* would preſent a Dozen unſully'd & untainted *Nymphs,* & Twelve of the moſt athletick & beſt-proportion'd young Men, to perform the celebrated Rites of Venus, in the ſalacious manner practiſed on the Iſland of *Otaheite* under the Tutelage of *Queen* OBEREA, in which Character Mrs. Hayes herſelf was to appear. Her Advertiſement met with much Approval, & ſhe was pleaſ'd to welcome no leſs than Three-and-twenty Viſitors on the allotted Evening, conſiſting chiefly of the Firſt Nobility, Baronets, & but five Commoners.

The Proceedings began at Seven O'Clock with the Preſentation to the *Nymphs* of a Nail, Twelve Inches in Length, in Imitation of the Gifts receiv'd by the Ladies of Otaheite from the Hands of lecherous Britiſh Sailors, Iron being prized highly by the Iſlanders. Thereafter, each Youth gave his *Nymph* a *Dildo-*ſhap'd Object, wreath'd in Flowers, & One Foot in Length. The Couples then copulated with remarkable Dexterity & Vigour, in a manner the Onlookers could not hope to emulate ! Theſe Exertions were accompany'd by ſuitable Muſick, & before long the Spectators had laſh'd themſelves into ſuch a Phrenzy of Laſciviouſneſs that they invaded the Floor, lay'd hold of the *Nymphs,* & gave their Paſſions free Rein ! They later refreſh'd themſelves with Bumpers of *Champagne,* & did not quit *Kings-place* until Four O'Clock in the Morning.

THAT CELEBRATED LADY ABBESS, MRS. JANE GOADBY,

So well-known to the *Nobleſſe,* having fitted up in the elegant *French* Stile for the refinement of our amorous Amuſements, her NUNNERY in *Marlborough-ſtreet,* has lay'd in

A Choice **STOCK of VIRGINS** for the Seaſon.

Her Eſtabliſhment is diſpoſ'd in ſuch uncommon Taſte, & ſhe has prepar'd ſuch an extraordinary Accommodation for Gentlemen of all Ages, Sizes, Taſtes, & Caprices, that it is judg'd it will far ſurpaſs every Seminary of the kind yet known in EUROPE.

The NUNS ſhe has engag'd are of the Firſt Rate *Filles de Joie* in *London,* the ſociety of whom only Men of Rank & Fortune might ſeek to enjoy. They are ſupply'd with Mrs. PHILIPS's Implements of Safety, & Mrs. GOADBY retains the Services of a Phyſician, who warrants that they are all found in Wind & Limb.

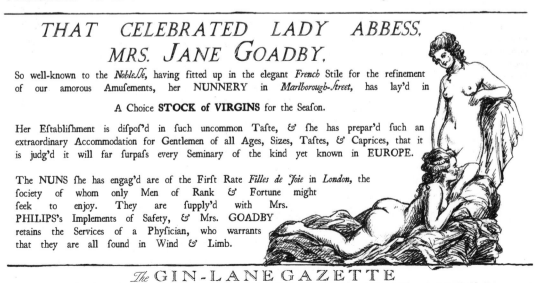

The SEVEN DIALS STROLLER

An Account of *The* FIGHTING PARSON's AFFRAY At *VAUXHALL-GARDENS.*

St. henry of Vauxhall, Defender of the LADIES.

THE *Reverend* HENRY BATE has shewn himself to be a Fellow who adheres more to the Teachings of the *Old* than to the *New Teſtament,* and who eſteems as his Text and Counſel the Precept an *Eye for an Eye,* over the Exhortation to turn the other Cheek.

Bate is the Rector and Squire of *St. Thomas's,* at *Bradwell-on-Sea,* in the County of *Eſſex,* and was taking a turn about *Vauxhall-gardens* on the 23rd Day of this Month with his handſome future Sister-in-law, the flame-hair'd Actreſs, Mrs. ELIZABETH HARTLEY, when that Lady found herſelf the Object of lewd Harangues from a Pack of faſhionable young Blackguards.

The Antagoniſts went on to avow that the Reverend Bate had inſulted their Confederate, one *Captain MILES,* the putative Friend and brawny Protector of the rowdy young Gentlemen, tho' I believe he is in point of fact a *Prize-fighter,* and Footman to the Ringleader, Mr. GEORGE ROBERT FITZGERALD.

It was ſettl'd that the Reverend Bate would defend Mrs. Hartley's Honour in a pugiliſtick Match at the *Spread Eagle Tavern,* and at this Eſtabliſhment he gave *Captain Miles* a SOUND BEATING. The Ruffian left with his face a *perfect*

Jelly, and Bate afterwards proclaim'd that Miles receiv'd in the ſpan of Fifteen Minutes *the Satisfaction he requir'd, not being able to diſcern a ſingle ray of Light, by which to find his way home,* ſo blacken'd and ſwollen were his Eyes.

The Confrontation has become known as *The Vauxhall Affray,* and is the ſource of great Amuſement amongſt the Quality. It ſeems a certainty that the *Heroick* Reverend's new *Sobriquet, The Fighting Parſon,* ſhall attach to him in Perpetuity. I underſtand that he nurtures Hopes of purſuing a Second Career as a Compoſer of Comick Operas, and a Third as a News-ſheet Editor.

1st JULY - HENRY FOX, 1st BARON HOLLAND of FOXLEY, departed this Life at Holland Houſe, at the Age of 68 Years.

In his final Days, Lord Holland on his Death-bed was viſited by his Friend Mr. GEORGE SELWYN, M.P. for *Glouceſter*, a Man known to cultivate an unhealthy Infatuation with DEATH in all its Myriad forms & Trappings, including Executions, Exhumations, Cadavers, & Coffins. When the *Necrophiliſt* Mr. Selwyn had excuſ'd himſelf from the ailing Man's bedſide, Lord Holland quipt to his Servant as follows :-

If Mr. Selwyn *calls again, ſhow him up : if I am alive, I ſhall be delighted to ſee him, & if I am Dead he would like to ſee me.*

It is believ'd that Lord Holland left this World having appropriated in exceſs of £400,000 from the Publick Purſe.

The Ghouliſh Mr. SELWYN

The Late Lord HOLLAND

Captain CONSTANTINE PHIPPS has the Honour of being the Firſt to deſcribe the Characteriſticks of the POLAR BEAR, in his Journal of A VOYAGE towards the NORTH POLE, undertaken by HIS MAJESTY's Command.

Capt. Phipps departed England in June of laſt Year, with Two Ships under his Command : HMS Racehorſe & HMS Carcaſs. Aboard the latter Veſſel was one Midſhipman HORATIO NELSON, who purſu'd a Polar Bear while the Carcaſs was entrapp'd in Ice, ſince he wiſhed to acquire its Pelt as a Gift for his Father. The Expedition ſail'd around Spitſbergen, & within 10 Degrees of the North Pole, but was oblig'd to turn about due to an exceſs of Sea-ice.

14th November -

A HIGHWAYMAN affail'd the Right Hon. FREDERICK AUGUSTUS, Lord BERKELEY, on *Hounflow-heath,* as that Gentleman ftruck out from his Houfe at *Cranford* to vifit Mr. Juftice BULSTRODE.

The Highwayman thruft in a Piftol at the Window of the Carriage, which His Lordfhip grafp'd & held afide, before prefenting & difcharging a larger Piece at the Ruffian, who fuftain'd a bloody Wound, & whofe Cloaths were fet ablaze by the Firearm's powder. The Felon rode fome diftance off, but was purfu'd, & was fhortly afterwards found dead. Two Confederates of the Highwayman then burft upon the Scene, but were feen off by His Lordfhip & his Servants.

The celebrated Mr. IGNATIUS SANCHO,

the Grocer, & Man of Letters & Mufick, is become the Firft BLACKAMOOR in *England* to enjoy the Privilege of Voting in a *General Election,* by virtue of being a Houfeholder of independent Means in the Ward of *Weftminfter.*

Mr. Sancho eftablifh'd his Premifes at 20 Charles-ftreet in January of this Year, after his Career as an Actor was curtail'd owing to a Weaknefs in his Speech. He was alfo Valet to the DUKE of MONTAGU, until an enervating & recurrent Gout oblig'd him to abandon his Pofition.

Eggs to throw at the Candidates? Twopence a Dozen!

30th November -

The HIGHWAYMAN JOHN RANN – known to the World as *Sixteen-ftring Jack* – has gafp'd his laft upon the Gallows at *Tyburn,* at the Age of 24 Years.

Rann had been employ'd as a Coachman before he embark'd upon his felonious Career, fince that humble Trade could not fatisfy his avaricious Proclivities. He was notorious for his regard for fine Apparel, & earn'd his *Sobriquet* owing to his Cuftom of tying Sixteen Strings to the Knees of his filk Breeches. Upon one Occafion, he attended *Bagnigge-wells* in a Coat of Scarlet, filk Stockings, & a lac'd hat, & having loft a gold Ring there, bragg'd that it was worth a trifling 100 Guineas, & that replacing it would be the work of but One Evening. Galling though it may be to allow it, Rann profecuted his criminal undertakings with great Swagger & Dafh, & Dr. SAMUEL JOHNSON has proclaim'd that *he tower'd above the common Mark* in his Trade. He was taken by the Judiciary upon feveral Occafions, but efcap'd Sentence due to the inability of Witneffes to confirm his Identity.

Rann's Miftrefs, one ELEANOR ROACHE, fought to pledge at a Pawn-broker's fome Moveables ftolen by him, & the *Bow-ftreet* Men were led to her Highwayman Sweetheart by this Error. Rann was vifited upon by countlefs Ladies in his Cell at *Newgate,* & gave a Dinner there upon the Eve of his Execution. He mounted the Scaffold before a cheerful & admiring Mob, attir'd in a Suit of Pea-green Cloaths, & fporting an extravagant Nofegay in his Buttonhole. He danc'd a Jig before the Rope was put about his Neck.

Sixteen to choofe from, Jack, my bonny Lad!

Of the late Mr. JOHN BASKERVILLE, Typefounder, & the SINGULAR MANNER of his BURIAL.

IT has come to our attention that the eminent Printer & Typefounder, Mr. JOHN BASKERVILLE, who died on the 8th Day of *January* laſt, was bury'd in an UPRIGHT POSTURE, at his own beheſt.

It was Mr. Baſkerville's wiſh as an Atheiſt that he ſhould be interr'd thus, within the Curtilage of his own Premiſes at *Eaſy-hill* – being unconſecrated Ground – in a Vault he had prepar'd expreſſly for the purpoſe within a conickal Building, which was heretofore uſ'd as a Mill. This he order'd as a Rejection of all Religion, ſince he evinc'd a hearty Contempt for Superſtition in general, & the Catholick *Barbariſm of Sure & Certain Hopes* of an Hereafter in particular.

In Life, Mr. Baſkerville's Godleſs Inclinations did not deter him from printing a much-admir'd *Folio* BIBLE in the Year 1763, & Mr. BENJAMIN FRANKLIN of the *Americkas* priz'd this eſtimable Letter-founder's Types to ſuch a Degree that they are employ'd in the printing of many Publications in thoſe rebellious Colonies.

SOLD BY
Mr. JAMES LEE & Mr. LEWIS KENNEDY

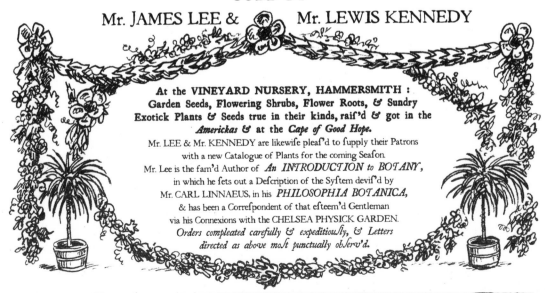

At the VINEYARD NURSERY, HAMMERSMITH :
Garden Seeds, Flowering Shrubs, Flower Roots, & Sundry
Exotick Plants & Seeds true in their kinds, raiſ'd & got in the
Americkas & at the *Cape of Good Hope.*
Mr. LEE & Mr. KENNEDY are likewiſe pleaſ'd to ſupply their Patrons
with a new Catalogue of Plants for the coming Seaſon.
Mr. Lee is the fam'd Author of *An INTRODUCTION to BOTANY,*
in which he ſets out a Deſcription of the Syſtem deviſ'd by
Mr. CARL LINNAEUS, in his *PHILOSOPHIA BOTANICA,*
& has been a Correſpondent of that eſteem'd Gentleman
via his Connexions with the CHELSEA PHYSICK GARDEN.
*Orders compleated carefully & expeditiouſly, & Letters
directed as above moſt punctually obſerv'd.*

The Gin-Lane Gazette

PUBLISHED in LONDON   *April, 1776.*   Nathaniel Crowquill Efq.

Particulars concerning the COUNTESS-DUCHESS, ELIZABETH CHUDLEIGH, & Her TRIAL for BIGAMY.

THE *Beau Monde* has lately prattl'd of naught elfe but the Trial of the bigamous ELIZABETH, COUNTESS of BRISTOL, which was attended by the Royal Family, Foreign Ambaffadors, & 6,000 of the Nobility & Gentry at *Weftminfter Hall.* It was a Spectacle which in its Magnificence & Beauty furpafs'd any Entertainment enjoy'd for many a Seafon.

It having been eftablifh'd that in the Year 1744 the Countefs – while Maid-of-Honour to the PRINCESS of WALES – had marry'd in fecret the EARL of BRISTOL, when that Gentleman was known by the lowlier Title of *Lieutenant the Hon.* AUGUSTUS HERVEY R.N., & that when that Match had fuffer'd an irreparable Breach fhe had fubfequently & bigamoufly marry'd the late DUKE of KINGSTON, it was refolv'd that fhe fhould be brought to anfwer for her Crime before 119 Peers of the *Houfe of Lords.* After Proceedings of Seven Days' duration, a Verdict of Guilty was pronounc'd unanimoufly, yet in claiming *Privilege of the Peerage,* fhe efcap'd the cuftomary Punifhment of Branding upon the Hand. She now purpofes to leave thefe fhores for *France.* The Earl of Briftol is reprimanded for his Part in perpetuating the Deception, & his Marriage to the Countefs is deem'd indiffoluble, with the inevitable Confequence that he fhall never fire legitimate Heirs. A Son born of his Match with the Countefs did not furvive beyond the Year 1747.

The DUKE of NEWCASTLE & his Party were feen to enjoy a fine Collation of fundry Meats, Wines, & Tea during the Trial. It was remark'd upon by all that the Countefs

IPHIGENIA'S LAST HUZZAH,

or, — The DUCHESS of KINGSTON attempts to relive paft Glories.

had loft the youthful Bloom & Pulchritude that had fo captivated her many paft Gallants, & that in growing ftout fhe had taken on a difpleafing Shape, refembling nothing lefs than a *Bale of black Bombazeen.*

Since fhe firft enter'd the Polite World as Mifs ELIZABETH CHUDLEIGH, the Countefs has prov'd herfelf a fhamelefs *Coquette* of the firft Water. The moft fcandalous of her Exploits is ftill fpoken of by the *Bon Ton,* & occurr'd in the Year 1749, when fhe attended a *Mafquerade* at *Ranelagh-gardens* in the Character of *Iphigenia,* Daughter to *Agamemnon,* attir'd in nothing more than diaphanous Gauze,

a Girdle of Flowers, & an arch Smile. PRINCESS AUGUSTA fought to conceal her Nakednefs with a Veil, but His Majefty KING GEORGE the SECOND evinc'd no fuch Scruples, enquiring of her if he might lay his Hand upon her Breaft. The faucy Jade reply'd that fhe would gladly direct the royal Paw to a yet fofter Place, & guided his Hand to his own Forehead. His Majefty was well-pleaf'd with this jape, & rewarded her with the Gift of a Watch worth 35 Guineas. Sixpenny Cuts of the Lady's comely Form were afterwards printed, & fold in great Numbers to her untold Admirers.

For fome time following the Death of the Duke of Kingfton, the Countefs made merry in *Italy* with the Fortune he had bequeath'd her. She attracted the lafcivious Attentions of *Pope* CLEMENT XIV, & others of the *Papal Court,* & her Yacht upon the *Tiber* was much admir'd by the Citizens of *Rome.* While the Countefs was engag'd in this foreign Jaunt, the late Duke's Nephew, & other Heirs, made it their bufinefs to prove that her Marriage was bigamous, being anger'd by the Terms of the Will. In her eagernefs to offer a Defence of her Actions in this Scandal, the Countefs threaten'd a fojourning Englifhman with a Piftol, to wreft from him the Price of her Paffage home.

Of Dr. THEODOR MYERSBACH, the PISS-PROPHET.

Mr. DAVID GARRICK has of late been fo greatly vex'd by unaffuageable Gout, & a Stone in his Kidney, that he has feen fit to feek Affiftance from the Urine-cafter, Dr. THEODOR MYERSBACH, a Man thought of by many as a canting EMPIRICK & MOUNTEBANK.

Dr. Myerfbach's Practice yields fizeable pecuniary Rewards, & it is faid that he is pleaf'd to treat Two-hundred Patrons each Day, many of whom are Peers & Gentry of the Firft Rank who pay Half a Guinea for the Quack's Pronouncements. His Income is faid to be 1,000 Guineas per Month, which allows him to satisfy his hankering after fine Cloaths, & to keep a Coach & Horfes. The Infirm vifit his new Premifes in Hatton-garden, & offer up Receptacles of Urine to the Medicafter, who examines their Water in the moft pompous & theatrickal Manner, before offering his *Diagnoſes.* He has been heard to boaft that by thefe Infpections alone he is able to determine the Age, Sex, & Hiftory of the Subject.

PISS PROFIT,
or, — The Mountebank's Pot of Gold.

This PISS-PROPHET had been a Clerk in a *Bavarian* Poft Office, before his arrival in *London,* where his Hopes of keeping Body & Soul together by means of becoming a Performer in an equeftrian Circus were dafh'd by a Deficiency in his Height. He foon fettl'd upon *Uroſcopy* as a certain path to Riches, having learnt fome Rudiments of Medicine from a Doctor who cur'd him of the Itch, & the great Number of credulous Boobies, fo befet by harrowing Diftempers that they trouble themfelves to hobble to his Door, fhews no Signs of diminifhing.

Of the FLAY'D CORPSE of a FELON, kept at the ROYAL ACADEMY.

THE eminent *Academician,* Signor AGOSTINO CARLINI, hopes to affift his artiftick Difciples in their Underftanding of Anatomy by the moft curious of Contrivances.

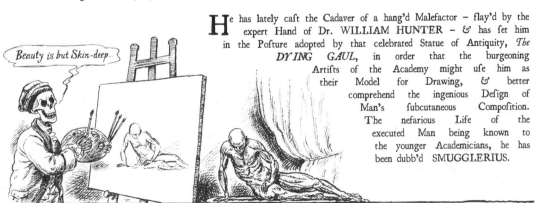

He has lately caft the Cadaver of a hang'd Malefactor – flay'd by the expert Hand of Dr. WILLIAM HUNTER – & has fet him in the Pofture adopted by that celebrated Statue of Antiquity, *The DYING GAUL,* in order that the burgeoning Artifts of the Academy might ufe him as their Model for Drawing, & better comprehend the ingenious Defign of Man's fubcutaneous Compofition. The nefarious Life of the executed Man being known to the younger Academicians, he has been dubb'd SMUGGLERIUS.

To the EDITOR:
SIR,

I write in connexion with your Notice of the SUICIDE of JOHN DAMER M.P., which appeared in your eftimable Publication for the Month of *Auguft.*

I am in a pofition to furnifh you and your Readerfhip with more compleat Particulars than heretofore fupply'd, and fhould have offered this Affiftance fooner, had not protracted bufinefs in *Derbyfhire* prevented me from fo doing.

Mr. Damer was an inveterate Gamefter and Spendthrift, whofe Profligacy brought about his Eftrangement from his fweet-natured Wife, the Sculptrefs, *Mrs. Anne Damer, née* Conway, and led him to amafs Debts, contracted with *Jewifh* Money-lenders and others, amounting to £70,000. I am told his Cuftom of attiring himfelf each day in Three new fets of Cloaths was a fource of fingular Exafperation to Mrs. Damer.

On the 15th of *Auguft* laft, Mr. Damer was lodged at the *Bedford Arms,* in *Covent-garden,* which he had frequented for many Years, and gave orders to *Mr. Robinfon,* the Landlord, that a Supper, Four Harlots, and a purblind Fiddler by the name of *Burnet* fhould be fent to his Room there. The Four Women fang while Burnet played until Three O'Clock in the Morning, whereupon Mr. Damer difmiffed the Party from the Room.

Some Hours later, Burnet became aware of a curious Smell emanating from Mr. Damer's Chamber, but took this to be nothing more than a fpilt Candle. When Mr. Robinfon later called upon Mr. Damer, he was greatly alarmed to difcover him lifelefs in his Chair, with blood at his right Temple, and a Piftol at his Feet. It was later thought that the Odour of the difcharged Weapon had been that which was miftaken for an upfet Candle.

The Verdict arrived at by the Inqueft convened that very Day was one of *Inftantaneous Death owing to Suicide* while being of a difordered Mind, and it was Mr. Damer's pecuniary Predicament that was thought to have unfeated his Reafon. I am reliably informed that Mr. Damer's Two Brothers are accruing fubftantial gaming Debts of their own, much to the Confternation of their Father, *Lord Milton,* whofe refufal to relieve his late Son's Burden muft furely have precipitated his felf-adminiftered Demife.

I am
Yours, *&c.*
S. L.
Weftminfter.

TILBURY FORT, ESSEX - This Month was arrang'd a GAME of CRICKET, in which the Counties of ESSEX & KENT were to play againft each other. There arofe a Difpute amongft thofe affembl'd as to the Eligibility to participate of one of the *Kentifh* Men, which foon broke into bloody Violence.

Firearms were purloin'd from the Guard-houfe of the Fort, & an Effex Man was fhot & kill'd by his *Kentifh* Adverfary. An aged Valetudinarian was transfix'd by a Bayonet, & in the courfe of attempting to reftore Order with Four other Soldiers, the Serjeant of the Fort receiv'd a Wound from a Bullet, & expir'd.

At this pafs, the Effex Antagonifts fled the fcene of Battle over the Draw-bridge, & the *Kentifh* Men made good their Efcape in Boats, moor'd at the Bank of the *Thames.*

Of Prepoſterous LADIES' FASHIONS, lately FRENCHIFY'D.

THO' they are ſatiriſ'd in publick Prints, mock'd in cauſtick Paragraphs in the News-ſheets, condemn'd from the Pulpits, & laugh'd at by every ſaucy Stripling in the Streets, the Ladies of Faſhion inſiſt upon perpetuating their ſlaviſh Devotion to Finery of prodigious & ridiculous Dimenſions.

The high Regard in which Abſurdities of Head-gear are now held is ſurely to be condemn'd as a *French Trait,* & is not one to be encourag'd in our Nation's Nobility & Gentry. Routs, Levees, & Balls are lately crowded with *Belles* who feſtoon their Hair with all manner of phantaſtickal Decorations, ſuch as miniature Ships, arrangements of Fruits & Feathers, & Birds who appear to have made their Homes atop their towering Treſſes. We hear often of Ladies who are oblig'd to ſit upon the floors of their Carriages, ſo tall are the Adornments perch'd upon their Scalps.

It is the caſe that the Bottoms of Ladies lately enjoy as much attention as their Tops, & the CORK RUMP is now employ'd under the Skirts, as an Enhancement to the female Poſterior. Perhaps we ſhould not yet be too haſty in cenſuring the modiſh Frivolity of thoſe wiſhing to cut a *Callipygian Figure,* ſince we have heard of an Inſtance this Month of a Lady's Life having been preſerv'd by ſuch falſe Buttocks. This Gentleman's Wife fell into the Sea during a boating Excurſion, but it prov'd impoſſible that ſhe ſhould ſink, owing to the Buoyancy of her CORK'D ARSE.

THE following, literally tranſcrib'd Hand-bill of a City Oculiſt demonſtrates that there are other brilliant decorations wanting, before the perſonal Charms of the modern Beau or Belle can be deem'd compleat !

CURIOUS ENAMELLED EYES,

Uſeful and ornamental, Upon an IMPROVED PLAN ;

Having the tone of action like life, is a great preſervation to the inner eye, worn with the utmoſt eaſe and comfort, acting like a glove to the hand, is a defence againſt colds, heats, duſt, &c. put into the head without pain, by John Watſon, at

W. Watſon's, Eye-builder, *Church-ſtreet, Coverly-fields, Mile End New-Town, London.* – Letters (poſt paid) duly anſwered.

Of the COUNTESS of DERBY's GAME of CRICKET, arrang'd folely for the LADIES.

THE DUKE of DORSET, & his lateft Paramour, the COUNTESS of DERBY, are fo enamour'd of CRICKET that they are eager to encourage Play amongft the female Sex. To this end, they have been pleaf'd to arrange a Game at the *Oaks*, in the County of *Surrey*, in which the Countefs, & Ladies of Quality & Fafhion alone were the Participants.

His Grace has made his Views upon the matter known in an Effay printed in a News-fheet, & he contends zealoufly that fuch a fporting Diverfion is fit for both Sexes. He urg'd the Ladies to caft afide their Needlework in favour of Cricket, & claim'd that they had lately demonftrated at the *Oaks* that they could handle a Ball & Bat as dexteroufly as any Gentleman. He went on as follows :-

What is human life but a Game of Cricket ? And, if fo, why fhould not the Ladies play it as well as we ? Beauty is the bat, and Men are the Ball, which are buffeted about juft as the Ladies' fkill directs them. An expert Female will long hold the Ball in play, and carefully keep it from the Wicket. When the Wicket is once knocked down, the game of Matrimony begins, and that of Love ends.

So numerous are the adulterous Attachments of the Duke that it feems certain he could himfelf field an Abundance of rival female Sides to contend with each other, without encountering infuperable difficulties.

Quite a Catch!

She moft affuredly is!

22nd Day of July - ANN MARROW was pillory'd at *Charing-crofs*, having been convicted on the 5th of the Month, at the *Quarter Seffions* of the City & Liberty of *Weftminfter*, of the vile Offence of going in a Man's Cloaths, & imperfonating a Man in Marriage with Three different Women, in the courfe of which fhe defrauded them of their Money & Effects.

The Difapprobation of the affembl'd Mob towards Marrow was fo great, that in pelting her with Ordure & Brickbats, fhe fuffer'd the lofs of her Sight in both Eyes. She muft alfo ferve a fpan of Three Months in Gaol.

Particulars concerning the EQUESTRIAN ENTERTAINMENT by Mr. DANIEL WILDMAN, & his celebrated EXHIBITION of BEES.

READERS unfamiliar with the fingular Performances of Mr. DANIEL WILDMAN will be aftounded to hear of his unequall'd Abilities, which have for yet another Seafon entertain'd the Publick.

Mr. Wildman firft exhibited his uncommon BEES in the Year 1766, & has fhewn them fince at *Dobney's Bowling Green,* Mr. *Aftley's Amphitheatre,* & at the *Colyfée* in *Paris.* He rides a Horfe ftanding upright, with one Foot upon the Saddle, & the other upon the Horfe's neck, all the while fporting on his Face a MASK of BEES. He might alfo be feen riding upright with the Bridle in his Mouth, & by firing a Piftol makes a Proportion of the Bees march over a Table, & the remainder of them fwarm in the air, before returning to their Hive again.

He can command Swarms to fettle inftantaneoufly wherever he pleafes, & orders them to alight upon his Head, or his Hand, or upon a Window. The following Lines moft appofitely encompafs the kindly manner in which he treats his wing'd Confederates :-

He with uncommon Art and matchlefs Skill,
Commands thofe Infects, who obey his Will ;
Bees others cruel means employ,
They take the Honey and the Bees deftroy ;
WILDMAN humanely, with ingenious eafe,
He takes the honey, but preferves the Bees.

An Account of the late DUEL with PISTOLS & SWORDS, fought by VISCOUNT du BARRI, & COUNT RICE.

THO' they had previoufly been upon very good Terms of the clofeft Friendfhip, Count RICE & Vifcount du BARRI lately fell into a Quarrel at *Bath,* in refpect of a gaming Tranfaction.

It being immediately refolv'd that Honour fhould be fatisfy'd with a Duel, the Two Gentlemen ftruck out for *Claverton Down,* with their Seconds & a Surgeon in attendance. Proceedings commenc'd at Dawn, & both Combatants were fupply'd with Swords, & a Brace of Piftols. The Piftols were employ'd firft, & the Vifcount was fhot in his Breaft, while the Count fuffer'd a Wound to his Leg. Firing a Second time, the Weapons fail'd to hit their Marks, & the Swords were taken up by the Duellifts. Upon engaging, the Vifcount dropt to his Knees, & begg'd of the Count, *Je vous demande ma vie !* The Count acquiefc'd to this Entreaty but, notwithftanding, his Opponent expir'd a fhort time after the Skirmifh.

The Coroner's Jury, conven'd to affefs this bloody Difpute, has return'd a Verdict of Manflaughter.

Of the WHOREMONGERING of LORD FUMBLE.

THE Depravities of General WILLIAM STANHOPE, the Second EARL of HARRINGTON, are well-known, but he has of late involv'd himfelf in a new Enterprife of Lewdnefs, as a Confequence of which the ftain of Notoriety fhall continue to befmirch his Reputation for fome time to come.

The Earl was a principal Patron of an Evening of debauch'd Venery at Mrs. SARAH PRENDERGAST's *Seraglio,* which he has been known to vifit in recent times upwards of Four times in any given Week. Mrs. Prendergaft offer'd a *Bal d'Amour,* to be attended by Subfcription, at which the fineft Women of Europe were to appear in *Puris Naturalibis.* The Earl was pleaf'd to favour her with a Difburfement of 50 Guineas, & brought his influence to bear in fecuring a further 700 Guineas from his diffipated circle of Friends.

Amongft thofe attending the *Soirée* were Ladies LUCAN & GROSVENOR, who difguif'd their Faces with Fig-leaves ; Mrs. GERTRUDE MAHON, the diminutive Cyprian, known as the *Bird of Paradife,* owing to her Predilection for gaudy Apparel ; & Mifs ISABELLA WILKINSON, the celebrated Rope-dancer & player of mufickal Glaffes at the *Sadler's Wells Theatre.* At the Evening's end, the Patrons are faid to have remov'd all their Cloaths, & enjoy'd dancing to Mufick fupply'd by an Orcheftra who play'd facing the Wall, that the Revellers might difport themfelves unabafh'd.

The Earl of Harrington, the Father of Seven Children, is a former Votary of Mrs. SOPHIA BADDELEY, & is known as both *The Goat of Quality,* & *Lord Fumble* due to his lecherous Nature. He keeps a *Harem* in his Houfe, which confifts of a Woman attir'd in the garb of claffical Antiquity, another cloath'd in a paftoral manner, & a Negrefs fporting a Turban.

Some Remarks upon the BED-TACKLE of
Mr. TENDUCCI, the CASTRATO.

INTELLIGENCE reaches us from *France* concerning Mr. GIUSTO FERDINANDO TENDUCCI, who has been far from idle fince his lateft Departure from thefe fhores in pecuniary Difficulties.

We hear that Mr. Tenducci was introduc'd to Herr WOLFGANG MOZART in Auguft, & that they have form'd a very amicable Attachment, to the extent that Herr Mozart was pleaf'd to compofe feveral mufickal pieces for the Caftrato to perform.

Mr. Tenducci's Marriage to his Wife DOROTHEA was annull'd in the Year 1776 as a Confequence of his lack of Potency, tho' he has claim'd to Signor CASANOVA that their Match yielded Two Children ! He explains this baffling Occurrence by defcribing how the Man who perform'd his Caftration in his Boyhood fail'd to detect that he was *triorchick,* by which it is meant that he was bleff'd with Three Tefticles at birth, & that his furplus & ferviceable Organ remain'd untouch'd by the Surgeon's Blade.

SRIPE PAWNBROKER

*What's all the Fufs ?
I've had Three Balls for Years.*

The Gin-Lane Gazette

PUBLISHED in LONDON — *April, 1779.* — Nathaniel Crowquill Esq.

An Account of the heinous PUBLICK MURDER of Miſs MARTHA RAY, Mother to NINE CHILDREN to the grieving EARL of SANDWICH.

THE EARL of SANDWICH is diſtraught beyond deſcription at the bloody Murder of his *Inamorata*, Miſs MARTHA RAY, at the *Covent-garden Theatre*, on the 7th Day of this Month. Having attended a Performance of Mr ISAAC BICKERSTAFFE's comick Opera, *Love in a Village*, Miſs Ray was leaving the Eſtabliſhment when ſhe was ſhot in the Head by Mr. JAMES HACKMAN, a Clergyman, who had nurtur'd an unſettling Infatuation with the Lady for ſome Seven Years. He made an attempt in the ſame Manner upon his own Life, immediately following his Aſſaſſination of Miſs Ray, but this prov'd unſucceſsful. He was ſeiz'd, & both he & the lifeleſs Lady were carry'd to the *Shakeſpeare Tavern*.

We are unable to corroborate the Rumours abounding that Miſs Ray & Mr. Hackman at one time enjoy'd a brief Amour, before the Lady broke their Attachment, to the Gentleman's acute Anguiſh. It is well-known, however, that Mr. Hackman & Miſs Ray were obſerv'd in a diſcreditable Situation by the *South-Seas* Iſlander, OMAI – Friend to Capt. JAMES COOK – during a Viſit by him to Lord Sandwich's Houſe. Mr. Hackman later ſought to impreſs upon

Mrs MARTHA RAY

Miſs Ray the Probity of his Character by relinquiſhing his military Commiſſion, & taking holy Orders, yet, notwithſtanding theſe Meaſures, the Lady perſiſted in ſpurning his Attentions. Mr. Hackman's jealous Regard for Miſs Ray led him to convince himſelf that ſhe had form'd a new Attachment to WILLIAM HANGER, Baron COLERAINE, when he ſpy'd her converſing with that Gentleman on the Night of the Murder. Miſs Ray's prolong'd Connexion with the Earl of Sandwich was likewiſe a ſource of unendurable Torment to him, & ſpurr'd him on to his deſperate Action. Mr. Hackman was ſentenc'd to ſuffer Death by Hanging, & danc'd the *Tyburn* Jig on the 19th Day of *April*.

Miſs Ray had been apprentic'd to a Mantua-maker of *Clerkenwell* in her youth, & the Earl is thought to have made her Acquaintance through the offices of the Procureſs, Mrs. HARDING. We underſtand that he pay'd her Father £400 for the liberty of taking her Maidenhead. The Earl's unfortunate Wife had ſuffer'd a diſorder'd Mind for many Years, & was made a Ward of the State in the Year 1767. Lord Sandwich & Miſs Ray liv'd for Eighteen Years in the Manner of Huſband & Wife at *Hinchingbrooke Houſe*, in the County of *Huntingdonſhire*, & ſhe bore him Nine Children. Miſs Ray evinc'd a great Talent for ſinging, & the Earl took it upon himſelf to have her train'd in the muſickal Arts by Meſſrs. BATES & GIARDINI. She was allow'd by all to be a Performer of prodigious Abilities, & ſang often the Works of the late Mr. HANDEL at *Hinchingbrooke*, where ſhe firſt met the lunatick Mr. Hackman, an Acquaintance of the Earl.

Miſs Ray was interr'd on the 14th *April* at *Elſtree*, in the County of *Hertfordſhire*.

———————————

Price: Fourpence

The SEVEN DIALS STROLLER

Particulars concerning the DUEL in *Hyde Park* between the Parliamentarians, Mr. CHARLES JAMES FOX, & Mr. WILLIAM ADAM.

I am never happier than upon thofe Occafions when I am able to bring you Tales of Courage, Honour, and good Breeding, and the late Duel fought by Meffrs. FOX and ADAM brings a tear of Admiration to mine jaded Eye !

A Difpute having arifen in the *Houfe of Commons* between thofe two Whiggifh Gentlemen concerning the ftate of affairs in the *Americkas* – during which Mr. Fox bellow'd at Mr. Adam, *Begone ! begone, WRETCH ! who delighteſh in libelling Mankind, in confounding Virtue and Vice !* – a Letter demanding Satisfaction was fubmitted to the unapologetick Fox by Adam, & Hyde Park was chofen as the Ground upon which the matter fhould be refolv'd. The Two Gentlemen were fupply'd with Piftols by Col. FULLARTON, and conven'd with their Seconds at Eight O'Clock on the Morning of the 29th November. The portly Mr. Fox had been counfell'd that he fhould ftand fideways before his Opponent, in order that he might prefent a fmaller Target, but in reply he quipt that fince he was as thick one way as another, this Expedient fhould be of little ufe !

Mr. Adam fuggefted to Mr. Fox that he fhould fhoot firft, but he refuf'd to do fo, ftating that fince he had no Quarrel with the Gentleman, that Honour fhould be his. Mr. Adam then difcharg'd his piece, and Mr. Fox return'd fire. It feem'd that neither man had fuffer'd Injury, and the Seconds enquir'd of Adam whether he was fatisfy'd. He ftated that he was not, and after Fox refuf'd to offer an Apology, Adam fir'd again, while Fox fhot his Ball into the air. The matter was then deem'd to be concluded, and Mr. Adam was pleaf'd to avow that his Antagonift had conducted himfelf with Honour.

It was then perceiv'd that Mr. Fox had fuftain'd a Wound, but this prov'd but a minor Injury to the Groin, and Mr. Fox will not be oblig'd to leave off wenching for any great fpell. He obferv'd that if Mr. Adam had not uf'd inferior Government Iffue Powder in his Piftol, he would furely have been kill'd. I have fince talk'd of the affair with Horrie Walpole, who fpeaks juftly when he declares that, of all Duels, this was the moft perfect, and that fo much Temper, Senfe, Propriety, eafy good Humour, and good Nature were never before fhewn.

I'll wager they are more accuftomed to ftabbing each other in the Back

PART the FOURTH
1780-1789

*M*y beloved Father once complain'd to me that the further a Man advances in Life, the greater will be the drains & checks on his Resources. These words were borne out, as my modest Success in Publick Life threw divers millstones around my neck, & I seem'd to accrue Dependants at every turn.

In 1783, my Sister's Husband was kill'd under the wheels of a Baronet's Curricle in *Towcester*, & I felt oblig'd to take on my young Nephew, Mr. HUMPHREY STROAKER, in the capacity of Apprentice *Gazetteer*. I own that I at first thought the Boy a feckless, ignorant Whelp, but resolv'd to afford him every Opportunity to better his lot & that of his poor Mother. I apply'd myself to his instruction with unwearying Zeal, & after a time his journalistick Capabilities flourished to a prodigious Degree. He demonstrated great skill in the rooting out of Gossip, & I suspect his handsome Countenance, & inveigling manner assisted in eliciting Intelligence from the comelier housemaids of Men of Rank & Fortune. I regret to say, however, that the Information he procur'd from these Belles de Nuit was not invariably of the strictest Veracity, & my *Gazette's* coffers were depleted by bothersome actions for Libel upon more than one Occasion.

Perhaps prompted by my young Protégé, Mr. Jakes rediscover'd his own wenching Proclivities, tho' his were of the sort demanding considerable pecuniary Expenditure, & I learn'd that he had taken to funding his nocturnal Profligacy by the most novel means. At this time, the *PRINCE of WALES*, & his debauch'd coterie of Libertines & Wantons, were notorious for their dissipation & free living. The young royal *Gallant* would offer a substantial purse to any Caricaturist who convey'd to him – *via* his fawning intermediaries – an Intention to publish a popular print portraying the Heir Apparent in a singularly Satirickal light. Mr. Jakes took full advantage of the Prince's Vanity, suppress'd many scurrilous Etchings, & lin'd his Pockets whenever he was able. Since this assisted the fellow in settling most of his Debts to me, & in no wise affected his duties at my Gazette, I turn'd a blind Eye to this perfidious Practise. Indeed, the Prince's Dissolution was meat & drink for my Readership, & both Jakes & I prosper'd to differing Degrees, courtesy of *His Royal Highness*.

*H*anoverian Turpitude notwithstanding, my Prosperity was not in any way assisted by the vigorous & domineering *Reverend BATE*. After a conviction for libelling *His Grace the DUKE of RICHMOND*, & finding that his position as Editor of the *Morning Post* had not remain'd open to him, he establish'd his own Periodickal, & his new *Morning Herald* soon became the dominant Scandal-sheet of our Age.

*F*or Ten long days in the Summer of 1780 there was fearful rioting by an *Anti-Catholick* MOB, the Turbulence & Violence of which struck TERROR into the Capital's heart. ——————

The Gin-Lane Gazette

PUBLISHED in LONDON   *June, 1780.*   Nathaniel Crowquill Efq.

An Account of the TERRIBLE CONFLAGRATION at Mr. LANGDALE's GIN DISTILLERY, begun by Lord GORDON's ANTI-PAPIST MOB.

THE City has not witneff'd Tribulations to match the late Riots – incited by the lunatick Anti-Papift, Lord GORDON – fince the terrors of the Great Fire, & no Crime at this prefent time, amongft the many perpetrated in proteft at the repeal of Laws governing *Catholicks*, was fo confounding as the wanton Pillaging & Deftruction of Mr. THOMAS LANGDALE's Diftillery.

Mr. Langdale's Popery had become common Currency, & the Mob having Intelligence that a *Papift* Chapel was to be found upon his Premifes in *Holborn*, march'd upon the Diftillery in great Numbers, at around 9 O'Clock on the Evening of the 7th of *June*. The Garrifon deploy'd there to defend Mr. Langdale, his Family of Twelve Children, & the Houfes of many of his Labourers, had been call'd away to fecure from attack the *Bank of England*. As a confequence, the Mob effected an unchalleng'd & violent entry to the Eftablifhment, & Papers, Furniture, & Chattels were foon pil'd up, & fet alight in the Street. A Fire was likewife begun within the Buildings themfelves, & a Wind got up, which ferv'd to fan the Flames into a terrible Inferno in a very little time. The blaze burft free of the Diftillery's Confines, confuming other Houfes in *Holborn*, & crept towards the *Fleet Market*.

Not content with this, certain Ruffians appropriated Two Fire Engines, & uf'd them to pump Gin from the Stills in the Diftillery's cellars, which they decanted into buckets, & fold for a Penny a mug to their riotous Confederates. Many of thefe did not wifh to pay for their Drams, however, & charg'd into the flaming Building in order to fill whatever they could find with Mr. Langdale's Gin.

The great Heat from the Conflagration took an infupportable toll upon the Stills, & they burft with a terrible force, driving the Gin upwards & into the Streets, where it ran down the Gutters. The turbulent Intruders were delighted at this, & threw themfelves to the cobbles in order that they might lap the fpirituous Rivulets into their Bellies. The Gin being unrefin'd & poifonous, it fear'd their Gullets, & thofe of their ragged-arf'd Wives & Children, & a hoft of convulf-ive, inebriated, & choking Scoundrels were to be seen rolling about in the Streets in Torment. Countlefs infenfible & ungovern-able People were trapp'd within the Premifes, & burn'd to death. A Vat holding 120,000 Gallons of Liquor was fet ablaze, its worth being eftimated at £38,000, & the *Vefuvian* Eruption this occafion'd was vifible within a compafs of Thirty Miles about the City, according to many of this News-fheet's Correfpondents.

The tardy Arrival of the *Northumberland* Militia reftor'd a little Order to the fcene, & they fir'd upon Pickpockets who were looting indifcriminately both the injur'd & the intoxicated, & the charr'd Corpfes of the demif'd.

Mr. Langdale's Loffes as a refult of this unparallel'd lawleffnefs are thought to amount to £100,000, & the Deftruction wrought upon the City as a whole, during the Ten Days of the Rioting, is grave beyond all poffible Defcription. Parliament, its Members, & Peers were befieg'd & attack'd, the King's Bench was raz'd to afhes, & *Newgate Gaol* was fack'd. 458 people are thought to have perifh'd or fuftain'd Injury, & 139 Felons have been taken by the Judiciary, not leaft amongft whom is the Prefident of the *Proteftant Affociation*, Lord Gordon himfelf, who is oblig'd to defend his life againft a Charge of High Treafon.

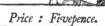

Price : Fivepence.

OF THE DUCHESS OF GORDON's ELECTORAL SKULDUGGERY.

NOT content with fomenting Riot & Rebellion in *London*, it seems that the *Clan* GORDON is now set upon perverting electoral Procedure. We are inform'd that the DUCHESS of GORDON, Sister-in-Law to the lunatic Anti-Papist Lord GORDON, has lately abducted an assiduous Champion of the Parliamentary Candidate Lord CAMPBELL, & has held him captive in a cellar in order that her preferr'd Aspirant, Capt. ELPHINSTONE, might enjoy the Advantage in his Campaign to win the Seat of *Argyll*.

Her Grace never has sought to suppress her zealous politickal Inclinations, & has prov'd a devoted friend to Mr. WILLIAM PITT in hosting Entertainments for the *Tories*, which have requir'd Disbursements from the Duchess of £200 upon each Occasion. If her Marriage to the DUKE of GORDON – known to his *Scotch* Compatriots as *Cock o' the North* – were a happier one, His Grace should perhaps display a little Rancour at her yet more intimate Friendship with Mr. HENRY DUNDAS, the *Keeper of the Signet* for *Scotland*.

The Duchess has ever been a spirited Wench, & it is averr'd that as a Child she was seen to ride a Pig through the Streets. She once suffer'd the loss of a Finger in the spokes of a Carriage wheel, & since that mishap has worn a Glove with a wooden Digit sewn into it.

Of Mr. de LOUTHERBOURG's beguiling EIDOPHUSIKON.

THE Publick has of late been greatly delighted by Mr. PHILIPPE JACQUES de LOUTHER-BOURG's Entertainment at *Leicefter-fields,* which he calls his *EIDOPHUSIKON.* He has employ'd his *myriad* Abilities – in the Defign & Conftruction of theatrickal Scenery – in the building of this wondrous Contrivance, in which the moft life-like Effects are wrought upon *tableaux* of Land & Seafcapes.

In his diminutive Theatre, a mere Seven Feet wide, Mr. de Loutherbourg prefents his Patrons with fundry Spectacles of Storms & Shipwrecks, Sunrife & Sunfet, Fire, & Thunder, by the Expedients of moving Scenery, miniature *Automata,* & varying Light, the whole being enhanc'd by mufickal accompaniments, & authentick effects of Sound. He has troubl'd himfelf to fabricate Foregrounds of Lichens & Mofs, which ferve to fortify the Illufion that the Spectator is looking directly upon a vifta of Nature. Views of the *River Thames,* & the *Bay of Naples* might alfo be feen. We are told that Mr. THOMAS GAINSBOROUGH is fo

entranc'd by the *Eidophufikon* that he is eager to build a fmaller Variant for his own & his Friends' Amufement.

Mr. de Loutherbourg was born at *Strafbourg,* & after receiving artiftick Tutelage at *Paris,* fettl'd in London in the Year 1771. He was employ'd by Mr. DAVID GARRICK at *Drury-lane,* who fo efteem'd his Proficiency in the Defign of Scenery that he was pleaf'd to offer him £500 *per annum.* Mr. RICHARD BRINSLEY SHERIDAN retain'd Mr. de Loutherbourg's Services when he took on the management of that Theatre, & had him devife & build Scenery for a revival of Mr. ISAAC BICKERSTAFFE's *Love in a Village.*

How do we know he has not fimply opened a Window?

Of Sir ASHTON LEVER's TOXOPHILITE SOCIETY, & HOLOPHUSIKON.

WE hear that Sir ASHTON LEVER, & his fellow Devotees of *Archery,* intend to eftablifh a TOXOPHILITE SOCIETY, in the Tradition of the Archers of *Finfbury,* & that it is their intention to practife the Bowman's Art in the grounds of *Leicefter Houfe.*

Sir Afhton Lever is a man of divers Taftes, as demonftrated by his eftablifhment of the *HOLOPHUSIKON* at *Leicefter Houfe,* which has delighted Patrons fince the Year 1775. This is a Mufeum of Curiofities, wherein are contain'd upwards of 25,000 Exhibits, comprifing preferv'd or ftuff'd Infects, Birds, Fifh, Reptiles, & Apes, & difplay'd Shells, & petrify'd Creatures & Relicts of antediluvian Antiquity. Alfo prefented for publick Scrutiny are fundry exotick Items donated by the eftimable Navigator Captain JAMES COOK. Patrons may gain admittance to delight in thefe Wonders for the Sum of 5s. 3d., or may wifh to purchafe an annual Ticket for 2 Guineas.

Sir ASHTON *acquires another* EXHIBIT.

PARTICULARS CONCERNING THE POISONING OF
SIR THEODOSIUS BOUGHTON, BY CAPT. JOHN DONELLAN.

2nd *APRIL* - Capt. JOHN DONELLAN was hang'd at *Warwick* for the Murder by Poifon of his Brother-in-Law, Sir THEODOSIUS BOUGHTON, after his Trial at the Affizes of that Town on the 30th of *March.*

Capt. Donellan – formerly of the *Royal Artillery* – became the Mafter of Ceremonies at the *Pantheon, Oxford-ftreet,* after he was cafhier'd from the Eaft *India Company* for pecuniary Mifdemeanours, & was marry'd to Mifs THEODOSIA BOUGHTON in June *anno* 1777. Sir Theodofius Boughton, her Brother of Twenty Years, would have become entitl'd to upwards of Two-thoufand Pounds upon his coming of age, & in the event of his Death, the preponderance of this Fortune was to accrue to the new Mrs. Donellan.

Sir Theodofius took Phyfick daily, & on the Morning of 30th *Auguft* laft, expir'd in Convulfions, with a terrible rattling in his Stomach, & foam at his Mouth, after imbibing a purging Draught that was later found to fmell powerfully of bitter Almonds. He was pronounc'd dead by Mr. POWELL of *Rugby,* an Apothecary.

An Error of prefcription by the Gentleman's Phyficians having been difcounted, fufpicion of Mifconduct fell upon Capt. Donellan. Following an Inqueft, a Poft Mortem inveftigation upon Sir Theodofius was undertaken by Dr. RATTRAY of *Coventry,* in fpite of the Corpfe's advanc'd ftate of Putrefaction. At the enfuing Trial, Dr. Rattray depof'd that the caufe of Death was moft affuredly a Poifon diftill'd from Laurel leaves, & it was known that Capt. Donellan was in poffeffion of the *Apparatus* neceffary for the fabrication of Laurel Water. Dr. Rattray alfo told the Court of Experiments with this Subftance undertaken upon Animals, & the mortal Effects thereof.

The eminent Doctor JOHN HUNTER fpoke againft the endeavours of Dr. Rattray in this matter, & told the Court that the Symptoms exhibited by Sir Theodofius were more likely thofe of an *Apoplexy* than of a Poifoning, but his Opinions were derided by Sir FRANCIS BULLER, the Judge prefiding. The Jury return'd a Verdict of GUILTY.

Capt. Donellan did not fee fit to confefs his bafe & infamous Crime upon the Gallows, & refuf'd to feek GOD's Mercy before he was turn'd off.

To the Victor, the LAURELS!

29th of **APRIL** - AT *All Saints' Church, at Burbage,* in the County of *Wiltfhire,* was chriften'd the Son of Mr. CHARLES STONE, a Tailor.

The Boy was nam'd CHARLES CARACTACUS OSTORIUS MAXIMILIAN GUSTAVUS ADOLPHUS STONE.

An Account of the disorderly MOCK-ELECTION of the DWARF, Sir JEFFREY DUNSTAN, as MAYOR of GARRATT.

THIS Month, a Mob of upwards of 50,000 Perfons attended the popular Mock-election of the Mayor of the Hamlet of Garratt, in the vicinity of *Wandfworth,* & the dwarfifh Dealer in old Wigs, JEFFREY DUNSTAN, fhar'd the Laurels with Sir JOHN HARPER as the fuccefsful Candidate.

This curious Spectacle of Derifion & Drunkennefs was firft held in the Year 1747, & its Infamy as a riotous Satire upon our Nation's electoral Syftem was fortify'd by the late Mr SAMUEL FOOTE's *Play The Mayor of the Garratt,* firft prefented at the Haymarket Theatre in the Year 1763.

Nine Afpirants advanc'd their Candidatures for the Poft of Mayor, amongft whom were the following, all having been afcrib'd entirely fpurious Names & Knighthoods :-

Sir JEFFREY DUNSTAN, aforemention'd ; one Sir CHRISTOPHER DASHWOOD, a Waterman, who rode upon a Boat fitted with Wheels, & drawn by Four Horfes ; one Sir WILLIAM SWALLOWTAIL, a Bafket-maker of *Brentwood,* who fat in a wicker Chariot, with a livery'd Servant in attendance ; Sir JOHN HARPER, aforemention'd, a Breeches-maker, who was carry'd in a Phaeton, & refrefh'd himfelf at every opportunity with a Bumper of Gin ; Sir BUGGY BATES, a Chimney-fweep ; & one Sir WILLIAM BLAIZE, a Blackfmith, whofe mount was a Cart-horfe, fitted with ears of Paper, reaching to the ground.

Upon thefe Occafions, the Candidates parade from *Southwark* to *Wandfworth,* where Scaffoldings are erected in the open air, & the multitudinous Mob gather in rowdy good Spirits, fome of them climbing Flag-poles in order that they might enjoy a more favourable view of the Pageant. Accompany'd by the *Garratt Cavalry,* being a company of Forty Boys upon Horfes of vary'd fizes, the Candidates then attempt to proceed to the Huftings at *Garratt,* but they are often prevented from fo doing by the great number of Carriages & Wagons impeding their paffage. The *Leathern Bottle Inn* at *Garratt,* & the wayfide Taverns along the allotted Road, are always happy Beneficiaries of thefe Gatherings, & the Ale-cafks of thefe eftablifhments invariably run dry.

The politickal Rivals then addrefs the Throng, & at this late Election, Sir Jeffrey & Sir John were unanimoufly return'd, & duly declar'd the Victors, tho' some mock Afperfions were caft upon the Probity & Impartiality of the former, when it was claim'd that one of his Daughters was betroth'd to the Prime Minifter, Lord NORTH.

Sir Jeffrey is a Foundling, who was taken in by the Workhoufe at *St. Dunftan's-in-the-Eaft,* before he was apprentic'd to a Green-grocer. He abfconded to *Birmingham,* where he found employment in the Manufactories, but return'd to *London* in the Year 1776, whereupon he began in the Trade of Wig-felling. Tho' he is but Four Feet high, he is efteem'd a Giant of Wit by his Friends, amongft whom is the radickal Mr. JOHN WILKES. The fame Wilkes, the late Mr. Foote, & the late Mr. DAVID GARRICK have penn'd feveral of the Addreffes made at the *Garratt* Elections, which often bemoan the Privations fuffer'd by the Lower Orders. Such is Sir Jeffrey's Popularity with his Electorate that his Likenefs appears upon Tokens & Inn figns.

The SEVEN DIALS STROLLER

Of Mr. WILLIAM HICKEY's good-natur'd HARLOT, & her Ability to PISS with Astounding ACCURACY.

YOU will never find a Fellow better acquainted with the moft frolickfome Women of the Town than Mr. WILLIAM HICKEY. He was pleaf'd to play Hoft on the 19th of laft Month to Lord FIELDING, & a Party of Roifterers, at the *Bull Tavern,* on *Shooter's Hill,* and made fure to invite only his moft intimate Circle of abandon'd Favourites, chief amongft whom was the incomparable Mifs PRIS VINCENT.

The ever full-bladder'd Mifs Vincent has a fingular Knack of fquirting her Wine acrofs a table, with fuch Precifion that fhe is able to fire into the neck of a Quart Bottle. Lord Fielding had heard claim that fhe poffeff'd fuch an Ability, but could not credit

Not of the oldeft Vintage, but I think you'll be amufed by its Cheekinefs...

it, and enquir'd of Hickey as to the Veracity of thefe Affertions. Hickey affur'd him that he had more than once feen her perform the Feat, whereupon His Lordfhip befeech'd him to arrange for the Party to witnefs it.

Hickey afk'd Mifs Vincent to oblige the Party with a Demonftration, and fince fhe had imbib'd a great Quantity of Wine, fhe readily affented, and defir'd Hickey to do her the Honour of being her Bottle-holder. He was happy to do fo, and took up a *Champagne* Bottle, while Mifs Vincent plac'd herfelf oppofite. He ftood at the fide of the Table, holding the Receptacle with its mouth in a flanting Direction toward her. Drawing up her Petticoats, fhe dexteroufly contracted and manipulated the lips of her Privities, fo as to produce a narrow Stream, which defcrib'd a graceful, golden arc fo correctly aim'd that at leaft One-third of her Water actually fill'd the Bottle.

Lord Fielding's Mirth at this fingular Accomplifhment was fo great that he was near Suffocation. Screams of Laughter likewife burft from the other affembl'd Three-bottle Strumpets, amongft whom were KIT FREDERICK, Mrs. TEMPEST, CHARLOTTE and NANCY BARRY, CLARA HAYWARD, and BET *The Blafted* WILKINSON.

Of young Master GRIMALDI, FLUNG into the PIT at SADLER's WELLS.

THE Son of the celebrated *Harlequin* & Dancer, Mr. JOSEPH GRIMALDI, lately efcap'd grave Injury by fome providence. The younger Jofeph is but Three Years old, & was attir'd as a Monkey for a Performance, during which his Father twirled him through the air at the end of a Chain. The Chain broke, & the Boy flew into the Pit, landing happily in the Arms of an aged Gentleman who was aftonifh'd to find himfelf embroil'd in the Entertainment.

The elder Grimaldi is fchooling his Son in the arts of the *Harlequinades,* but he is a fevere Teacher, known to many as *Grim-All-Day.* He is alfo known as *Iron Legs,* & acquir'd this Name at *L'Opéra Comique* in the City of Paris, when he leapt onto the Chandeliers at that Theatre to win a Wager. He was once vifited by the DEVIL in his Dreams, who told him that he would die on the Firft Friday of a Month unfpecify'd, & he is known to keep Vigil on thofe Days, fhutting himfelf in a Room full of Clocks, where he gibbers until Sunrife. He alfo fears that he will be bury'd alive, & his Will makes clear that his Head fhould be parted from his Body by his Daughter, Mary, before his interment.

OF THE COITAL & PROGENITIVE
DR. JAMES GRAHAM'S GRAND

THE Begetting of Heirs has ever been a Duty of the Nobility, & Dr. JAMES GRAHAM offers Hope to those amongst the Quality whose Loins are not as fruitful as they might wish them to be. He has lately establish'd new Premises for his *GRAND STATE CELESTIAL BED*, at *Schomberg House, Pall-Mall* – which he stiles his *Temple of Hymen* – & for a Price of Two Guineas, both the Childless & the idly Curious may gain admittance to witness the modish Diversion of this modern *Elysian Palace.*

His Temple is bedeckt in the most lavish manner imaginable, & greets the Eyes of its Visitors with gilded Looking-glasses, Statuary, Crystals, Garlands, Perfumes, distant Musick, & gold & silver Ornament in such profusion that it dazzles with the Light it reflects. Posture Molls – which he calls his *Goddesses of Youth & Health* – are in attendance, & a *Nymph*, in a state of *deshabillé*, disports herself in the guise of the Goddess *Vestina.*

In these Surroundings, & for a Price of 5 Shillings, Dr. Graham is pleas'd to give his celebrated Lectures on the venereal Act, in which he lays great Emphasis upon the import of electrickal Fire as an Aid to blissful & fecund Coition. At the conclusion of his Orations, an electrickal Shock is given to his Visitors by means of Conductors, which are conceal'd under the cushions of their Chairs. A Shade, or Spirit, of prodigious size & haggard Visage, is seen to emerge from the floor of

Mr. BENJAMIN FRANKLIN

Dr. GRAHAM has long sought to surround himself with People of Rank & Influence, & is doubtless delighted to welcome such Notables as His Royal Highness The PRINCE of WALES, Her Grace The DUCHESS of DEVONSHIRE, the EARL of SANDWICH, Mr. CHARLES JAMES FOX, Mr. JOHN WILKES, & Mrs. MARY *Perdita* ROBINSON to *Schomberg House.* His near Neighbour in Pall-Mall is the celebrated Mr. THOMAS GAINSBOROUGH.

Dr. Graham was born in *Edinburgh*, & has liv'd in the Americkas, where he establish'd a successful Practice, & in *Philadelphia* he learn'd much of Mr. BENJAMIN FRANKLIN's Experiments with electrickal Fire. He return'd to these Shores in the Year 1774, & offer'd his Services as an Oculist at *Bath.* The celebrated Historian, Miss CATHERINE MACAULAY, became one of his most favour'd Patrons in that City, & she has marry'd the good Doctor's Brother.

INVIGORATION AFFORDED BY STATE CELESTIAL BED.

the Room, & gives a Bottle of Liquor to the Doctor, who ſhows it to the Company, before it is again carry'd away by the Apparition. A young Woman in the Character of the Goddeſs of Muſick then ſings ſix Songs, before ſhe too takes her leave.

The *Celeſtial* or *Magnetico-electrickal* Bed is recommended to his Audience as a certain & inſtantaneous Cure for Barrenneſs, & for the Sum of £.50, any Gentleman & his Lady deſirous of Progeny may enjoy a Night in the *Celeſtial Apartment.* The Bed is 12 Feet long by 9 Feet wide, & ſupported by 40 Pillars of Glaſs, of variegated colours. The Dome of the Bed pours forth odoriferous & balmy *Arabian* Eſſences, while at its Summit are plac'd living Turtle-doves upon a Bed of Roſes, & Three Figures, of *Cupid, Pſyche,* & *Hymen,* the Torch of the latter burning with electrickal Fire. The Dome likewiſe carries an Orcheſtra of *Automata,* which plays ſweet Muſick upon Flutes, Horns, Guitars, Violins, Oboes, & Kettle-drums. At the Bed's Head is an Organ, before which is a Landſcape in miniature, containing moving Figures of a Marriage Party, proceſſing into

a *Temple of Hymen.* The whole Contrivance moves upon a Pivot, & may be fix'd in an inclin'd plane. It is alſo ſet about with Lodeſtones, the 15 cwt. of which pour forth a magnetick tide of majeſtic *Effluvium,* in an ever-flowing Circle. The Sheets are of the ſofteſt Silks, & ſtain'd in colours to compliment the Complexions of his Patrons. The Mattreſs is fill'd with ſpringy Hair, procur'd at great expenſe from the Tails of good Engliſh Stallions. By theſe means he hopes to propagate a Race of Beings ſtrong in mental & bodily Endowments, to populate the terraqueous Globe.

Dr. Graham aſſerts that the ſuperior *Ecſtaſy* which Couples may enjoy in the Celeſtial Bed exceeds anything yet known in the World, & that in being agitated powerfully in the Delights of Love, the unprolifick will ſurely fulfil the Commandment emblazon'd upon his Invention, & ſcintillating with electrickal Fire :

BE FRUITFUL, MULTIPLY, AND REPLENISH THE EARTH.

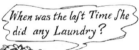

When was the laſt Time ſhe did any Laundry?

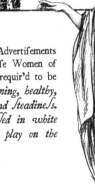

UPON occaſion, Dr. Graham has been oblig'd to place Advertiſements in the News-ſheets for a new or additional Goddeſs, & we adviſe Women of the Town ſeeking Employment in the Temple of Health that they are requir'd to be *genteel, decent, & modeſt* ; they muſt be *perſonally agreeable, blooming, healthy, and ſweet tempered and well recommended for modeſty, good ſenſe and ſteadineſs.* The Goddeſs is to live in the *Phyſician's family,* to be daily dreſſed in white ſilk robes with a rich roſe coloured girdle, & if ſhe can ſing, play on the harpſichord or ſpeak French greater wages will be given.

NEWS from our CORRESPONDENT at BATH, Mr. HENRY SANDFORD Efq.

OF AN ATTEMPTED MURDER BY MISSIVE.

A N anonymous and villainous letter was directed to and received by the Rev. ALEXANDER ADAMS, of *Belton, Somerfet,* on Friday the 22nd of this Month, in which the author ftated : *The great regard I have for you induces me to take this neceffary, tho' ftrange Method of fending you what I firmly believe will be the Means of making you an ufeful member of Society, from which at prefent you feem to be debarred.* He went on thus : *I will tell you plainly what Remedy I have fent, which is Nothing more or lefs than a little decoction, which I would advife you to fwallow, or, if that is not so agreeable, only to fnuff it up your nofe the moment you receive it, and I make no doubt but it will have the defired effect. To prevent you having any Doubt of the Ingredients, it is only the juice extracted from the SMALL-POX of a fine, buxom country lafs.*

The letter was figned *Juvenis,* and addreffed from Brandon Hill, on the 18th of the Month. It appears to have been fent with a defign of taking away Rev. Adams's life, and a Reward of twenty guineas is offered by that Gentleman to any perfon who will difcover the perpetrator. The original, which is ftained with a yellowifh Tincture of a naufeous fmell, is left and may be feen at the rooms of Mr. RIDLEY's, Surgeon of *Penford.*

A DUST IN WET WEATHER IN THE CRESCENT, OR BATH IN UPROAR.

M rs. MACARTNEY – known to our City as *Mother Mac* – gave a ball and fupper of late, during which fome of the young Gentlemen attending perceived that a fingle bottle of Claret had been conveyed privately to a Peer of *Papift* inclinations, and determined that Commoners fhould partake of the cup alfo. Wine was called for, yet Wine was denied ! The clamour reached the ears of the crabbed hoftefs, who approached the company with her eyes rolling about like balls grinding Muftard feeds in wooden bowls. *My cellar doors, Gentlemen* (faid fhe), *are locked, and thofe who will not go up and dance are defired to walk out of my houfe !* This was not complied with. Glaffes were broke, and the bare-picked drumfticks and pinions of the roafted fowls ferved to the Party were thrown about. The confternation of the hoftefs and the company became general. Madame la Comteffe de ——— thought that officers of the police were come to take her prifoner to the *Tower,* and half a dozen Scotch ladies of Quality hid themfelves in an Ice-clofet ! I have oft heard of revels being broke up due to too much Wine, but rarely have I heard of diforder erupting from too little.

W hat a fad picture is *Mother Mac* of Human nature ; a Termagant worn down with Age, and without a friend, who can find no better way to beftow her ample fortune than in giving entertainments, balls, fuppers, routs, drums &c. to a variety of genteel people. Confider, *Madam Mac,* how many poor wretches you might make happy with your bounty, inftead of feafting the rich !

T he lady is infamous in our City for her promifcuity, drunkennefs, and ungovernable choler, and fhe browbeats her vifitors into accepting her invitations. Miss FANNY BURNEY has damned her as *bold, hardened, painted, fnuft, leering and impudent,* and Mifs Burney's friend, Mifs COOPER, avers that fhe is *one of the worft women breathing : a Drunkard notorioufly, an affiftant to the vices of others, and an infamous practitioner in all fpecies of them herfelf.*

Mr. SANDFORD Efq.
No. 1 *Royal Crefcent, Bath.*

VOTARY
of
Venus

WE PRESENT TO OUR READERS OUR BOLD CYPRIAN FOR THE MONTH OF MAY, MRS. MARY PERDITA ROBINSON.

A former Difciple of Mr. GARRICK, Mrs. MARY ROBINSON was once the *Inamorata* of the PRINCE of WALES – who play'd *Florizel* to this celebrated Actrefs's *Perdita*, till his roving Eye fettl'd upon Mrs. ARMISTEAD – & her matchlefs Allurements have been enjoy'd by the incorrigible Libertines, Mr. CHARLES JAMES FOX, & Col. BANASTRE TARLETON, & admir'd in France by the DUC de CHARTRES, & Queen MARIE ANTOINETTE.

H er cornuted Hufband is a fecklefs Debtor, & *Perdita* was once feen by the Audience of the *Covent-garden Theatre* to haul him by his Hair to the Veftibule, & to rain down violent blows upon him, after fhe had obferv'd him paying lafcivious Attentions to another young Lady in a Box. She alfo exhibited this fpirited afpect of her Character in feeing off a Footpad, who accofted her as fhe was ftriking out in a Phaeton acrofs *Hounflow-heath,* to vifit her inconftant Prince at *Windfor.*

W e hear that this Month, a young Gentleman fought Ten Minutes' *Converfation* with *Perdita* for the Sum of Twenty Guineas, & that when fhe affented, he haften'd to her Houfe to enjoy what he hop'd would be a vigorous Tumble in the Bed-chamber. He was chagrin'd beyond words when he was ufher'd into her prefence, & found her feated with a mirthful Col. Tarleton & Lord MALDEN. She honour'd the Bargain by affording her Votary precifely Ten Minutes of Converfation, before taking his Twenty Guineas, & ringing for her Servant, who fhew'd him out.

The SEVEN DIALS STROLLER

OF THE CORPSE OF MRS. EMILY POTT, FORMERLY WARREN, TOW'D BEHIND A VESSEL IN INDIA BY HER GRIEVING HUSBAND.

A moſt affecting Account reaches me of the ſudden Demiſe of one of our moſt celebrated *Belles*, the former amorous Fair Mrs. EMILY POTT, Wife of Capt. BOB POTT of the *Eaſt India Company*.

Pott and Emily ſail'd from *Madras* for *Calcutta* in May, at a time when the Lady was ſuffering with the Prickly Heat, which is very prevalent in *Aſia*. Being tortur'd by this Complaint, and having an inſatiable Thirſt upon her, ſhe took to imbibing draughts of ic'd water mix'd with milk, and after taking two ſuch Tumblers, complain'd of a ſudden faintneſs, Nauſea, and failing Sight. She fell in a Swound upon a Couch, and within the ſpan of a few Moments expir'd. Bob was ſo ſhock'd at this Calamity that he could not for many Hours be perſuaded that ſhe had periſh'd.

The ſwift blackening and noiſome Putrefaction of Emily's Cadaver preſented Bob with incontrovertible proofs of his Wife's death, however. A Coffin was prepar'd for her, and once encloſ'd therein, ſhe was plac'd in a Boat aſtern of the Ship, and tow'd with a long rope to *Calcutta*. There ſhe was interr'd in the Town's ſacred Burial-ground, beſide the *River Hooghly*, and at an Expenſe of near Three Thouſand Pounds, Bob had a ſtately *Mauſoleum* conſtructed over her Grave by Mr. TIRETTA, the Architect. He alſo commiſſion'd Mr. Tiretta to build a commemorative Column at an additional coſt of a Thouſand Pounds — amongſt the Tigers of *Culpee*, in the Vicinity of which place his beloved had departed this Life.

Emily was the Daughter of a blind Beggar, and was taken in by the Bawd, Mrs. CHARLOTTE HAYES, when ſhe was but Twelve Years old. Mrs. Hayes was ſtruck forcibly by the uncommon Beauty of the Child's Countenance, and ſaw that her Eſtabliſhment at *King's-place* might profit by her charms. Mrs. Hayes ſchool'd her in the Arts of Venery, but Emily never learn'd reading or writing. Her picture was taken by Sir JOSHUA REYNOLDS, who lauded her handſome Figure as much as any Man. She came under the Protection of Mr. WILLIAM HICKEY, Mr. COVENTRY, Mr. WARREN, and Mr. CHARLES GREVILLE. She firſt became acquainted with Bob Pott in the Year 1776, who made her a Wanton in High-keeping, and houſ'd her in *Cork-ſtreet*. To his Father's great Diſpleaſure, he endow'd her with her own Carriage, in bright yellow, and with Pott's Arms reſplendent upon it, livery'd ſervants to command, and a Box at the Opera.

REMARKS UPON THE
EROTICK HABERDASHERY OF THE DUC DE CHARTRES.
BY MR. H. STROAKER.

AS a vifitor to our fhores, it is conceivable that the DUC de CHARTRES is unaware of the courtefy the *Englifhman* extends to the Ladies of his acquaintance by keeping his lecherous predilections to himfelf.

The *Frenchman* attended the races at *Newmarket* earlier this month, and fported on his coat a fet of large and exceptionable buttons, that gave great offence to feveral Ladies on account of the fubjects exhibited upon them. Each carried a frolickfome little Device, in which divers beafts were fhewn in the throes of phrenzied copulation. Amongft the creatures difplayed were a dog upon a bitch, and a ftallion covering his mare.

I fee His Grace is buttonholing the Ladies again...

This obfcene Haberdafhery is now the talk of every Salon in town, and is remarked upon by Ladies in countlefs letters to their friends and relations, in the moft difapproving tones. This fhould demonftrate to our *French* gueft that when the delicate Senfibilities of *Englifh* Females fuffer a fhock, it is the cuftom to remedy this by difperfing its effects as widely as poffible.

WONDERS ! WONDERS ! WONDERS !
DR. GUSTAVUS KATTERFELTO

is very glad that the *King, Queen,* and all the Royal Family, and many of the firft Nobility, have exprefled the higheft fatisfaction in feeing his GRAND PERPETUAL MOTION. EVERY DAY this Week, from ten till fix, he will fhew and explain his various new Machinery of Perpetual Motion, that the public at large may fee its myfteries. He will admit every Lady and Gentleman for 2s. each, tradefmen 1s. only.

Alfo, by his new-invented SOLAR MICROSCOPE, 15,000 live *Infects* will be feen, as if as big as a large eel, in a drop of beer the fize of a pin's head, and 40,000 live *Infects* in a drop of clear water, the fame number in milk, vinegar, and blood ; alfo live caterpillars, appearing to the eye to be as large as an ox, and as rough as a bear ; and 800 other uncommon objects which cannot be feen by any other Solar Microfcope, which is now exhibited from eleven till three O'clock.

Dr. KATTERFELTO This and Every Evening, precifely at eight O'clock, will alfo deliver one of his popular lectures, and will entertain his audience with many grand deceptions on dice, cards, billiard, letters, money, watches, &c., and his wonderful and moft furprifing BLACK CAT will appear again in a moft aftonifhing manner.

The admittance at night is front feats 3s., fecond 2s., back 1s. only, at No. 24, Piccadilly.

Of Mr. CHARLES JAMES FOX's ESSAY on FARTING.

IN feeking to win a confiderable Wager by penning an *Effay* on Wind, Mr. CHARLES JAMES FOX, M.P. – its rumour'd Author – has undertaken to claffify the feveral Species of FARTS, thus fparing *Natural Philofophers* the trouble of grappling with this odious tafk themfelves.

This fingular work is humbly dedicated to the Lord CHANCELLOR, & Mr. Fox afferts that he has heard from feveral of His Lordfhip's fellow Peers that he farts, without referve, when feated upon the *Woolfack,* in a full affembly of Nobles. Mr. Fox goes on to avow that there are Five or Six breeds of Fart, which are perfectly diftinct from each other, both in Weight & Smell :- *Firft,* the fonorous and full-ton'd, or roufing Fart ; *Second,* the double Fart ; *Third,* the foft, fizzing Fart ; *Fourth,* the wet Fart ; and *Fifth,* the fullen, wind-bound Fart. If Mr. Fox undertook Experiments in this branch of Study at *Brooks's Club,* where we believe the Wager was contracted, we truft he faw fit to do fo in the abfence of naked Flames.

The allurements of Speculation have taken hold of Mr. Fox to fuch a degree that he is frequently oblig'd to live off the Charity of his Friends, & in May of 1781, his goods & chattels were auction'd to fettle his Debts, & he was taken in to the home of Mr. Mann, an Apothecary. His perpetual Bankruptcy cannot be wonder'd at, when one recalls fuch inftances of his Profligacy as his being embroil'd in a Houfe-fire, & laying bets with his Friends as to which burning Roof-beam would be the firft to collapfe.

He is now fchooling his rakifh Friend, the PRINCE of WALES, in whoring & pecuniary Diffipation, & His Royal Highnefs has this Year feen *Parliament* fettle his Debts, which amounted to £30,000. It is amufing to confider that Mr. Fox was inftrumental in both leading the Prince aftray, & in brokering an Accord with the KING, whereby the Royal Firft-born is to receive £50,000 *per annum* from the royal Purfe, a capital fum of £60,000, & revenues accruing from the Duchy of *Cornwall,* amounting to £12,000 *per annum*. It feems unlikely that the Prince fhall be able to live within thefe means, however, & he has already order'd lavifh Improvements to his refidence, *Carlton Houfe,* which is condemn'd by fome as *a perpetual fcene of Excefs.*

Of Sir JAMES LOWTHER, EARL of LONSDALE, & his Attachment to his DECEAS'D PARAMOUR.

THE EARL of LONSDALE has once again fhewn that his Sobriquets of Jemmy Grafp-all, Wicked Jimmy, & the Earl of Toadftool are not attached to him without good caufe, by his ill-ufage of his Attorney & Agent, the late Mr. JOHN WORDSWORTH of Cumberland. The Earl never once remunerated Mr. Wordfworth for the various fervices he render'd, & he ow'd the Gentleman at his death a fum amounting to fome Four or Five Thoufand Pounds.

Damn it, Man! There's a Fly in my foup!

The Earl has ever been a peculiar Fellow, & this has never been better demonftrated than by his actions towards the Daughter of one of his Tenants. He made her his Paramour, & worfhipp'd her with fuch ardour, that when fhe of a fudden died, he could not bear to be parted from her, & notwithftanding her encreafing Putrefaction, kept her Body in Bed, or had her cloath'd & fat at his Table. When fhe had moulder'd to a degree the Houfehold could no longer endure, he plac'd her in a glafs-topt Coffin, which he kept in a Cupboard, before he at laft faw fit to have her bury'd in the Cemetery at Paddington.

The Gin-Lane Gazette

PUBLISHED in LONDON   *July, 1784.*   Nathaniel Crowquill Esq.

An Account of the Attempt made by The Prince of Wales upon his Own Life, & his Hopes of wooing Mrs. Maria Fitzherbert.

8th of JULY - Tormented by sharp Pangs of unrequited Ardour for Mrs. MARIA FITZHERBERT, His Royal Highness, the PRINCE of WALES, stabb'd himself with a Sword at *Carlton House.* His Wound was dress'd with Bandages, which he threaten'd to tear off, unless the Object of his Affections came to him without delay.

The Love-sick Prince has lay'd relentless siege to Mrs. Fitzherbert since *March* of this Year, but the Citadel of her Honour has heretofore remain'd unbreach'd. This desperate late Action caus'd the Lady to yield, however, & she hurry'd to her injur'd Suitor in the company of the DUCHESS of DEVONSHIRE. The Two Ladies were shewn into the royal Presence, & were greeted with the sight of the bawling Prince flopp'd upon a Sofa, with bloody bindings about his Breast. He declar'd that nothing would induce him to live unless she consented to marry him, which she agreed to do, against her better Judgment. The Prince sought to seal the Accord with a Ring, & the Duchess gave up one of her own for the purpose. Mrs. Fitzherbert then excus'd herself, & quit *Carlton House.* The Lady was soon

overcome with Regret for having made such a foolhardy Promise in such circumstances, & made Arrangements to decamp to *France* without delay. His Royal Highness now importunes Mrs. Fitzherbert to return to him, in pitiable Letters oft amounting to more than Forty pages, & vows that if she will not assent to come hither, *he* shall be forc'd to go to *her.*

The Prince has suffer'd no permanent harm to his Person, tho' we cannot speak for his heavy Heart, which he permits to rule his disorder'd Head in this matter to the extent whereby he believes that matrimonial Union with the

Roman Catholick Mrs. Fitzherbert will be greeted with Felicity & Junketing by his censorious Father. Moreover, the *Act of Settlement,* the *Act of Union,* & *the Royal Marriages Act* – the latter prohibiting any descendant of the late King GEORGE the SECOND from marrying without the Permission of the King – will surely prove insuperable Obstacles to a lawful state of Wedlock being contracted between the Prince & his wavering Lady-love.

Mrs. MARIA FITZHERBERT is by Six Years the Prince's elder, & demonstrates both an uncanny Knack of accruing Husbands, & a singular Inability to retain them. Her First Spouse, Mr. EDWARD WELD, died in the Year 1775, when he fell off his Horse, & the Second, Mr. THOMAS FITZHERBERT, expir'd at *Nice* in the Year 1781, from a Distemper he acquir'd at the time of Lord GORDON's Riots. The injur'd Prince seems undeterr'd by these ill Omens, and it must have been a great Novelty indeed for the Lady to see a Suitor so near Death *before* any Nuptials have been perform'd.

Price : Fivepence.

The SEVEN DIALS STROLLER

OF THE ECCENTRICITIES OF MR. THOMAS GAINSBOROUGH.

A long-ferving Retainer in the Houfehold of Mr. THOMAS GAINSBOROUGH fupplies me with the moft diverting Intelligence concerning his Eccentricities and working Methods.

Mr. Gainfborough has been a Member of a Mufick Club in *Ipfwich,* the gatherings of which oft become exceffive merry. The Artift has been the Butt of many Japes upon thefe Occafions, and his Wig is fometimes fnatch'd from his Head and thrown about the Room. His drinking exceeds all Temperance, and he has been known to be incapable of working for a Week afterwards.

Suffolk's Sons are Plain-fpeakers, it feems, for while his Rival, Sir JOSHUA REYNOLDS, fawns fhameleffly over Drury-lane's moft celebrated Actrefs and Beauty, Mrs. SARAH SIDDONS, Mr. Gainfborough was heard to fay of her – while engag'd in taking her Likenefs – *Damn the Nofe ! There's no end to it !* Others fortunate enough to fit for him are furprif'd by Mr. Gainfborough's

curious working Methods. It is his Cuftom to place his bemuf'd Sitters befide his Eafel, to ftand away from the Canvas, and to fketch out the Portrait ufing Brufhes which are an aftounding Six Feet in length. He alfo builds Landfcapes in miniature, employing them as the Models from which he paints, with Cork and Coal as Rocks, Sand and Clay as Earth, *Broccoli* as Trees, and fherds of Looking-glafs, which ferve for reflective bodies of Water. One of his *Fancy Paintings* requir'd the portrayal of Swine, and for a fpell Mr. Gainfborough kept Three Piglets in the Studio of his *Pall-Mall* Houfe, which might be feen fkipping about his Feet as he work'd.

Mr. Gainfborough was once introduc'd to the late Dr. SAMUEL JOHNSON by the late Mr. GARRICK, but the Encounter left the Artift with an unfortunate Affliction. The literary *Leviathan* was an infamous Twitcher, bedevill'd by nervous Tics, and following an Evening in the Doctor's company, Mr. Gainfborough acquir'd fome of thefe Habits himfelf. He complain'd that he fancy'd himfelf turn'd into a *Chinefe Automaton,* condemn'd inceffantly to fhake his Head, and for a Month or more was unable to keep ftill, while afleep or awake.

OF THE WONDERFUL LEARNED PIG.

Mr. NICHOLSON is now pleaf'd to fhew his remarkable LEARNED PIG at the *Sadler's-wells Theatre,* following its unequall'd Succefs at *Dublin, Nottingham, Scarborough, York, &* the *Charing-crofs.* The Beau Monde will wait for Hours for an opportunity to fee him, & fo popular has he prov'd that other Performers at the Theatre threaten to quit their Situations, rather than fee themfelves rank'd upon the Play-bills as Inferiors to SWINE.

This fagacious Animal folves *Arithmetickal* problems by picking up cards with its mouth, is able to reckon the Number of People prefent, can tell the Time by a Watch, fpell Words, & diftinguifh Colours, & can read the Thoughts of Ladies in the Audience.

There is much Debate concerning the true Capacities of the Pig's Wits, & the late Dr. SAMUEL JOHNSON offer'd his Opinions laft Year, ftating : *The Pigs are a Race unjuftly calumniated.* Pig has, it *feems, not been wanting to* Man, *but* Man *to* Pig. *We do not allow Time for his Education ; we kill him at a Year old.* The following lines are publifh'd upon the matter :-

Though Johnfon, learned BEAR, is gone,
Let us no longer mourn our lofs,
For lo, a learned HOG is come,
And Wifdom grunts at Charing Crofs.

Happy for Johnfon that he died
Before this Wonder came to Town,
Elfe had it blafted all his Pride
Another Brute fhould gain Renown.

OF THE SALONS OF WIT,
HOSTED BY THE BLUESTOCKING, PROFESSOR S—R—H C————LL.
BY NATHANIEL CROWQUILL.

MANY Gentlemen of my acquaintance aver that the Ladies can be moſt engaging Wits, yet when I hear talk of any *Blueſtocking* who is reputed to evince Qualities of Humour, Erudition, & Scholarſhip, I am reminded of the late Dr. SAMUEL JOHNSON's celebrated Obſervation that a Woman preaching is like a Dog walking on its hind Legs : *'Tis not done well, but you are ſurpriſ'd to find it done at all.* For my part, I have long been of the Opinion that a *learned Lady* is as novel as a *learned Pig* – or as rare in the World as a Hog that ſprouts wings & flies.

It was with many Miſgivings, therefore, that I accepted a cordial Invitation to attend one of the frequent *Salons* hoſted by S-R-H C-------LL, a Lady lately arriv'd in our City from the renegade Colonies of *America.* The Gentlemen of her Circle favour her with the Title of *Profeſſor,* & tho' it is common knowledge that our former Dominions have cultivated many eccentric & confounding Cuſtoms in recent Years, we have heard no creditable reports that even their ſchools at *Harvard* or *Princeton* are become ſo lunatick as to permit Women to enter the rever'd Halls of *Academe,* much leſs to inſtruct in them. I can only conclude that her ſuppoſ'd Title is a ſatirickal one.

I viſited the *Lady Profeſſor* at her ſurpriſingly elegant Rooms in inelegant *Soho* – tho' as One of late from the Colonies ſhe muſt have accuſtom'd herſelf to making the beſt of the rudeſt & meaneſt Surroundings. On the allotted Evening, I found not a cloſ'd Society for the recondite, but a Salon with its Doors flung open to anyone of Wit, Culture, or Learning. A pert Female of the *Beau Monde* might rub ſhoulders with the well-bred Man ; the virtuous Matron with the merry Coxcomb. Furthermore, the Lady herſelf is in no wiſe what we have been led to believe a *Blueſtocking* ſhould be – her Stockings are not Blue, & her Hair is dreſſ'd in the higheſt Faſhion. When I ventur'd a ſally that we do not expect to find either Americans or Ladies much intereſted in Book-learning, ſhe tapp'd my Arm with her Fan, & chided me for allying myſelf with the late Dean SWIFT : *For,* quoth ſhe, *Did he not aſſert that a pernicious Error prevails, & that it is the Duty of my Sex to be Fools ?* She warm'd to her Theme : *Surely it were better that all Humankind ſhould aſpire to Wiſdom, above*

Ignorance. Our little Society has been miſrepreſented ; we meet for the ſole Purpoſe of Converſation ; we do not play at Cards, but at Ideas. And unlike the Gentlemen of our acquaintance, we are ill-diſpoſ'd to reſtrict our Company to either the frailer or the ſtronger Sex. Indeed, we hold that Learning may be found in the moſt ſurpriſing of men – aye, & in the Ladies too. We attend rather to the quickeſt of Tongues & readieſt of Wits, to whomſoever they belong.

The Profeſſor refuſ'd, during our unfortunate Spat with our Colonies, to vouchſafe to her *Engliſh* Intimates whether ſhe was a Revolutionary, or loyal to the Britiſh Crown, & for ſuch a forthright lady, ſhe exhibited a ſudden Coyneſs when I enquir'd into her Politicks. Yet, for a *Blueſtocking* & a Colonial, ſhe is aſtoniſhingly couth, & welcomes any to her Salon who might wiſh to participate in the Converſation. With the Promulgation of her Cauſe in mind, ſhe & her Circle have favour'd my humble *Gazette* with their moſt generous Patronage, & before I knew what ſhe was about, ſhe had coax'd from me an Aſſurance that I would eſpouſe their Cauſe within its pages ! That Duty is now happily diſcharg'd.

An Examination of the FASHION

SINCE there has been in this Nation for upwards of a Twelve-month a very great Fashion in AERIAL VOYAGING, we offer to our Readers a Survey of the most entertaining Histories of this modish Diversion.

OF MR. VINCENZO LUNARDI's BALLOON.

THE Publick's Preoccupation with Balloons was engender'd by Mr. VINCENZO LUNARDI, of *Lucca,* in *Tuscany,* who was the First Aerial Traveller in Britain, & ascended into the Heavens from the *Artillery-ground* at *Moorfields,* on the 15th Day of September last. It seem'd that the Populace of *London* in its entirety was assembl'd to witness this astonishing Enterprise, with the PRINCE of WALES the Principal onlooker.

Accompanying Mr. Lunardi on his Voyage was a Dog, a Pigeon, & a Cat, the latter becoming nauseated during the Flight, obliging the intrepid Italian to descend briefly, & to entrust the Creature to the care of a Girl, in a field at *Welham Green.* The Balloon's Course took it above the County of *Hertfordshire,* while Mr. Lunardi din'd upon Chicken, & quaff'd Champagne, & upon occasion convers'd with Farm-hands below, with the aid of a Speaking-trumpet. He regain'd *Terra Firma,* after Two and a Half hours, at *Thundridge,* near the Town of *Ware,* tho' his Landing was not without difficulties, & the Anchor with which he hop'd to secure the Machine prov'd as ineffectual as the Oars he had put aboard for the purposes of steering his Craft. It was only with the Assistance of a handsome Milkmaid – the fearful local Menfolk having refus'd to come to his Aid – that he was able to bring the Bouncing Contraption to rest. The celebrated Mr. Lunardi is now at the Meridian of his Glory, & he has been honour'd with the Hospitality & Plaudits of the *Bon Ton.* His Balloon was exhibited at the *Pantheon,* in *Oxford-street,* to universal Acclaim, & a Medal was struck to commemorate his Accomplishment.

Of EXPERIMENTS by OTHER GENTLEMEN in BALLOON FLIGHT.

A country Surgeon, Mr. EDWARD JENNER, launch'd a Balloon from the Court-yard of *Berkeley Castle,* in the County of *Gloucestershire,* on the Afternoon of the 2nd of September last Year. The Machine floated for Ten Miles in a North-Easterly direction, descending at *Kingscote.* In retrieving it, Mr. Jenner made the acquaintance of Miss CATHERINE KINGSCOTE, upon whose Father's Estate the Balloon had come to rest. We understand that Mr. Jenner & Miss Kingscote have form'd an amatory Attachment, & Marriage is talk'd of.

Dr. ERASMUS DARWIN has hopes of establishing an Aerostatick Balloon Post, & in *January* of last Year made an attempt to float a Balloon from *Derby* to *Soho, Birmingham,* but was thwarted in this Endeavour by an unkind Wind. In *January* of this Year, Messrs. JEFFRIES & BLANCHARD made a Flight across the *English Channel,* descending at Calais.

The Opportunities for Mischief that Balloons afford has not been overlook'd by roguish Urchins, & aerial Contrivances made of Paper, & fuell'd by flaming wads of Wool drench'd in spirituous Liquids, are launch'd with alarming regularity, & pose a great Hazard to the Nation's Hay-stacks.

for EXCURSIONS in AEROSTATICK BALLOONS.

Of Mrs. LAETITIA ANN SAGE, the First FEMALE AERONAUT.

THE publick Clamour for further aeronautickal Entertainments led Mr. Lunardi to arrange a Second Flight, on this Occafion in the Company of Mr. GEORGE BIGGIN, Col. HASTINGS, & the Actrefs & noted Beauty, Mrs. LAETITIA ANN SAGE. The Balloon was emblazon'd with a *Union Flag,* & inflated before a boifterous Mob at *Newington Butts, St. George's Fields.*

It was foon found that the Weight of the Paffengers – that of Mrs. Sage being not the leaft confiderable – hinder'd the Balloon's Afcent, & it was decided that Mrs. Sage & Mr. Biggin alone fhould have the Honour of exploring the Atmofphere.

The Voyage took them along the Courfe of the *Thames.* They enjoy'd a light Repaft, & encounter'd an unfeafonable Snow-ftorm, before defcending at Harrow, where they were abuf'd to a favage degree by a Farmer, whofe Hay they had flatten'd. A Party of Boys from *Harrow School* rufh'd to their Affiftance, however, placating the Farmer with a Purfe of Money, & efcorting the Aeronauts to an Ale-houfe, where their Adventure was toafted moft intemperately.

There has been much Conjecture as to whether Mrs. Sage & Mr. Biggin celebrated their Succefs in a more amorous manner, while aloft.

Mrs. SAGE

O! my Lord! It goes up fo eafily!

Of a LEWD WAGER.

IT feems that the Thoughts of fome Gentlemen have turn'd very quickly towards the Poffibilities of Aerial Debauchery, as the following line enter'd in the Wager Book of Brooks's Club attefts :-

Lord Cholmondeley has given two guineas to Lord Derby, to receive 500 guineas whenever his lordfhip fucks a woman in a Balloon one thoufand yards from Earth.

Of the TRADE in BALLOONIANA.

THE *Beau Monde* is ever ready to fhew its Admiration for fafhionable Accomplifhments, & now do fo by purchafing all manner of Trinkets, emblazon'd upon which are depictions of Aeroftatick Balloons. Such goods as Hat-pins, Stick-pins, Snuff-boxes, Brooches, Plates, Fans, Vafes, & popular Prints are fold in great Quantities, & Ladies are feen in Dreffes ornamented with Balloon Defigns, & even go fo far as to wear the moft extravagant Balloon Hats. The Organift of *St. Clement Danes,* Mr. THOMAS SMART, enjoys great Succefs with his new Song, *The Air Balloon.*

The Gin-Lane Gazette

PUBLISHED in LONDON   *August, 1786.*   Nathaniel Crowquill Efq.

AN ACCOUNT OF THE ATTEMPT MADE UPON THE LIFE OF THE KING BY A MAD WOMAN.
BY MR. H. STROAKER.

2nd of AUGUST - AT *St. James's Palace*, HIS MAJESTY's Perfon was fubjected to an attack by a woman brandifhing a knife. The King evinced fingular fortitude and compofure, however, and he was unharmed by the lunatick, who has now been carried to *Bedlam*.

His Majefty was to attend a Levee at the Palace, and as he alighted from the royal coach, the woman gave him a paper. He was pleafed to accept it, thinking it perhaps to be a petition, and as he bowed gracioufly to her, fhe twice thruft her blade at him, the fecond ftrike cutting his waiftcoat a little. She was feized, and the King expreffed fome concern at the rough ufage fhe fuffered at the hands of his attendants, faying, *Do not hurt her ! She has not hurt me. The poor creature appears to be infane.* The weapon was afterwards found to be a fruit-knife with a cracked, ivory handle, and fo worn thin was its blade that it could never have pofed a grave threat to His Majefty's life.

Before enjoying the Levee as he had planned, the King gave ftrict orders that the Queen was not yet to be troubled with news of the affault, and upon returning to *Windfor* he told Her Majefty what had occurred, and demonftrated to her chearfully that he was wholly unharmed. The royal Daughters and the Queen were greatly fhocked by the news, and fhe took His Majefty's hand, ftating moft movingly, *I have you yet !*

The King's affailant is identified as one MARGARET Peg NICHOLSON, and a fearch was made of her lodgings, in which were found demented writings ftating her rightful claim to the nation's throne, and her avowal that *England will be difcharged with blood for a Thoufand years* if her claims were not publickly acknowledged.

Her cafe has provoked much deliberation as to what the nature of her fate fhould be, and difcovers a weaknefs in our laws with regard to how beft the Judiciary fhould deal with thofe who commit crimes while fuffering the taints of infanity. Were

fhe to be pronounced mad, fhe fhould be fet at liberty, but the fafety of a troubled Publick might be placed in jeopardy. Were fhe to be tried and convicted of an attempt upon the King's life, fhe fhould moft affuredly hang for her Treafon. It has fallen to the *Privy Council* and Lord SYDNEY to adjudicate in this matter, and it has been found that Mrs. Nicholfon is indeed infane, and it is ordered that fhe fhould be confined to *Bedlam* for the remainder of her natural life. It is ftipulated that fhe fhould be taken care of, and fhould be engaged there in whatever ufeful employment fhe is capable of in order to fupport herfelf. We have heard complaints that *Bedlam* has never before been ufed as a *Government* hofpital for the deranged, and if it were to be confidered as fuch, fome new wings fhould be conftructed to accommodate the numberlefs lunaticks who fet ftore by *Government* promifes.

Mrs. Nicholfon is now in the care of the ftewards of the Hofpital, and fhe fubmitted to her confinement calmly and without complaint, her only enquiry about her new circumftances being when fhe would have the pleafure of a vifit from the King.

Price: Fivepence

The SEVEN DIALS STROLLER

REMARKS UPON MR. WILLIAM BECKFORD's NEW NOVEL,
& HIS ILLICIT & INFAMOUS AMOUR WITH MASTER COURTENAY.

WHILE moſt Sodomites are content to ſatisfy their unnatural Compulſions within the Confines of the Molly-houſes, Mr. WILLIAM BECKFORD did not ſcruple about conducting his ſcandalous Intrigue with a Boy of Ten Years old within the auguſt edifice of a Country Houſe, but, as a conſequence of his Reckleſſneſs, he was oblig'd to flee theſe ſhores in Diſgrace. He perſiſts in granting his debauched Mind untramell'd licenſe, however, and has lately publiſh'd a Volume entitled *Vathek, An Arabian Tale,* which is replete with *Gothick* epiſodes of Luſt, and unſpeakable Inceſt. He claims to have compleated his Work within the compaſs of Three Days and Two Nights, which I aſſume conſtituted as long a ſpan at his *Bureauas* he could endure, without enacting the Imaginings of his diſeaſ'd Fancy in real Life.

Mr. Beckford firſt made the acquaintance of the Son of the EARL of DEVON, Maſter WILLIAM Kitty COURTENAY, in the Year 1779, and was ſtruck forcibly by his handſome Viſage, deſcribing the Boy as *A young Divinity.* The ſcene of their ſubſequent amatory Attachment is rumour'd to have been *Powderham Caſtle,* near *Exeter,* and it afterwards came to the attention of the Boy's Uncle, Lord LOUGHBOROUGH, who ſought to diſcredit Beckford, and leave his politickal Aſpirations in ruins, by publiſhing in a News-paper the intimate Correſpondence of the Two befotted Williams. Beckford's name was beſmirched beyond Redemption by the enſuing Scandal, and he ſoon

decamp'd to the Continent with his Wife, the former Lady MARGARET GORDON, who died after bearing a Child in May of this year. He was deny'd the Honour of a Peerage by His Majeſty the KING, who heartily wiſh'd him hang'd.

Beckford's mode of living has been an egregiouſly extravagant one, ſince he celebrated his coming of Age in *September* of the Year 1781. Having inherited at Nine Years of Age a capital ſum of £1,500,000 from his late Father, and an Income of £70,000 *per annum,* he reſolv'd to enjoy his pecuniary advantages to the full, and the Entertainments at his Twenty-Firſt Birthday Celebration laſted for Three days. The Fireworks, banqueting, Wines, Italian Singers of Opera, and the decorative Contrivances deſign'd and built by Mr. PHILIPPE de LOUTHERBOURG requir'd Diſburſements of £40,000. He has likewiſe lay'd out a Fortune on *Gothick* Improvements to his Seat of *Fonthill Abbey,* in *Wiltſhire,* which has ſince become known as *Splendens,* reflecting its new and ſingular Opulence.

Beckford departed for *Italy* in the Year 1782, with a Retinue of Valets, Cooks, Footmen, and Muſicians in attendance, charg'd with the Duty of ſhielding him from the many Privations of foreign Travel. So great was his *Entourage,* and ſo long was his Baggage-train of Books, Prints, Furniture, Plate, and Cutlery, that at *Augſburg* he was miſtaken for the *Emperor of Auſtria* making his way to Rome to viſit the Pope.

OF THE PROPHET POORHELP, & HIS PROGNOSES GOT BY PALM-LICKING.

THE lateſt QUACK to impoſe himſelf upon a credulous Publick is SAMUEL BEST, who calls himſelf *Poorhelp*, & numbers the BISHOP of DURHAM, & the KING himſelf amongſt his Patrons. He ſhares an Apartment in the Workhouſe at *Shoreditch* with a Bantam Cock, & a ſmall Child known as *Lord Cadogan*, and he prognoſticates there upon the future Health & Diſtempers of his Viſitors by the method of licking the Palms of their Hands. His Walls are bedeckt with celeſtial Devices, & a Picture of JOHN WESLEY. He gorges upon bread & cheeſe, & Gin mix'd with Tincture of Rhubarb, & ſuppoſes himſelf to engage in nightly Conſultations with the Archangel *Gabriel*. He propheſies that the World will come to an end by the Year 1950, & if this Publication's Succeſſors are ſtill to be found ſupplying our Readers' Progeny with News in 163 Years, they ſhall doubtleſs be pleaſ'd to keep them inform'd of the manner in which *Doomſday* plays itſelf out.

PRITHEE, Now WASH YOUR HANDS

OF THE FENCING MATCH BETWEEN MONSIEUR DE ST. GEORGE – THE BLACK MOZART – & THE CHEVALIER D'EON, OF UNCERTAIN SEX.

*C*arlton Houſe, *9th of April* - The PRINCE of WALES, Mrs. FITZHERBERT, and others enjoyed a fine exhibition of ſwordſmanſhip by M. de ST. GEORGE & the CHEVALIER d'EON, the latter gaining a deciſive victory. M. de St. George is of *African* deſcent, and is allowed by all to be the beſt ſwordſman in *France*. He is the firſt Blackamoor to attain the rank of Colonel in that nation, and commanded a regiment of 1,000 Blackamoor volunteers. His talents as a *Virtuoſo* of the violin, and compoſer of muſick, are likewiſe greatly eſteemed.

Does my Bum look big in this?

*T*he CHEVALIER d'EON firſt arrived in *England* in the year 1763, having been recruited to the *Secret du Roi* by King LOUIS XV, who beſtowed upon him the *Order of St. Louis* for ſundry diplomatick ſucceſſes. The *Chevalier* adopted women's cloaths in the courſe of his duties, and has ſince ſhewn reluctance to caſt them off. *Signor* CASANOVA was perſuaded that he was a woman, and ſo authentick is his female character that there was much ſpeculation on the *London Stock Exchange* as to his true Sex. An enquiry into a wager on the matter was conducted by the CHIEF JUSTICE to the *Court of King's Bench*. The *Chevalier* was affronted by theſe indignities, and challenged many a coffee-houſe ſtockjobber to a duel. The *Secret du Roi* being diſbanded on the death of the King, the *Chevalier* entreated his French maſters to allow his return. This was permitted, but on the unaccountable condition that he ſhould live for the remainder of his days in the character of a woman. He aſſented to this, but ſtipulated that the Government ſhould ſupply him with new ſets of women's cloaths. He preſented himſelf to the *French* court, having firſt enjoyed a *toilette* laſting four hours at the hands of a ſervant to Queen MARIE ANTOINETTE. He was then gaoled after being ſeen in men's cloaths, before returning to England in the year 1785, whereupon he once again took on the guiſe of a *luſty dame*, in which character he ſeems happieſt. Tho' 59 years old, he travels widely, giving demonſtrations of fencing to a bewildered but admiring Publick.

17th **of April** - The PRINCE of WALES was likewiſe pleaſ'd to arrange a pugiliſtick Conteſt at *Barnet* fought by Mr. DANIEL MENDOZA, & Mr. SAM MARTIN. Mendoza defeated Martin in leſs than Thirty Minutes, a Feat made all the more remarkable by his being but 5ft., 7ins. in height, & weighing but 160lbs. His ſingular Method of blocking blows, ducking, ſide-ſtepping, & dancing about, is condemn'd by ſome as cowardly, tho' not by his royal Admirers, & ſhould he be favour'd with an Introduction to the KING – as is lately propoſ'd – he ſhall be the firſt *Jew* to have that Honour.

Mr. MENDOZA

Of PRINCELY CHAGRIN at the RIDICULE of Mrs. FITZHERBERT's ARSE.

I afk you! What's remotely funny about THAT?!

WE have heard of late through Mr. JOHN WILKES that the PRINCE of WALES has inftructed his Lawyers to profecute Mr. SAMUEL FORES, of the Printfhop at No.3, Piccadilly, for the Publication in July of Two calumnious Caricatures. One of the cuts is by the hand of Mr. JAMES GILLRAY, & fhews what is thought to be a true Incident : His Royal Highnefs & Mrs. FITZHERBERT are thrown violently from their *Phaeton,* the *bare Arfe* of the latter being expof'd to publick fcrutiny as her Skirts tumble over her head, while the face of the former is on the point of burying itfelf in the ample Rump.

The SEVEN DIALS STROLLER

An Account of The PRINCE of WALES & Major HANGER RACING TURKEYS against GEESE.

DURING a riotous gathering at *Carlton Houfe,* Major GEORGE HANGER held forth on the relative perambulatory merits of the Goofe and the Turkey, and concluded that the Turkey was the better traveller. The PRINCE of WALES fet great ftore by this Opinion, and a Wager for £.500 was ftruck with Mr. BERKELEY in refpect of a race for Birds over Ten Miles.

Mr. Berkeley having felected an excellent Party of Geefe, Major Hanger was deputed by His Royal Highnefs to procure Twenty of the fineft Turkeys that could be had, and on the allotted Day the Gentlemen ftruck out for the Starting-poft to fettle the matter. The Turkeys held the lead for Three Hours, advancing as they had a full Two Miles ahead of their Rivals, but as Night came on, the Turkeys began to look towards the Trees at the

Road-fide, and roofted therein. Barley was ftrewn upon the ground, while the Prince attempted to drive them on ufing a Pole, to which was attach'd a red Cloth, and Major Hanger was able to diflodge one of their Number from the Branches, but thefe defperate meafures avail'd them nothing.

Mr. Berkeley's Geefe foon came waddling on, and paff'd the Turkeys, who refolutely rebuff'd all

attempts to expel them from their arboreal Shelter. The Geefe were declar'd the Victors as a Confequence.

Of GIN, BEER, & MONEY'D BUG-CATCHERS at St. THOMAS's & GUY's HOSPITALS.

THE eminent Mr. JOHN HOWARD has fet about writing an Account of the principal Hofpitals in *Europe,* and we are privy to fome of his findings with refpect to GUY's and St. THOMAS's.

Mr. Howard complains that prodigious quantities of Beer are brought into the Hofpitals for confumption by the infirm, and that fpirituous liquors are likewife carried there from the adjoining Gin-fhops, all of which has injurious effects upon the efficacy of diet and medicine in thofe eftablifhments.

Mr. Howard has alfo found that in feveral of the older wards at Guy's, the wooden bedfteads have not yet been replaced with iron ones, and are infefted to an alarming degree with lice. The Hofpital's chief bug-catcher is afforded a wage of £.40 *per annum,* which is equal to thofe of the Surgeons, and if this fum were expended in airing, beating, and brufhing the beds, his infupportable falary might be all but difpenfed with.

PARTICULARS CONCERNING MR. THOMAS WHALEY'S WALK FROM DUBLIN TO JERUSALEM, FOR A SIZEABLE WAGER.

LIKE many of his fellow Countrymen, the egregiously diffolute *Dubliner,* Mr. THOMAS *Buck* WHALEY, is infamous for enjoying a frolickfome Wager, & the greater its eccentricity, the better difpof'd he will be to undertake it.

Mr. Whaley readily owns that he was *born with high Paffions, a lively Imagination, and a Spirit that could brook no Reftraint.* Upon one Occafion, he jump'd from the Window of his Drawing-room, fituated on the Second Floor of his Houfe on *Stephen's-green,* into the firft paffing Carriage, & kiff'd its Occupant. Upon another, he leapt his Horfe from the fame Window, & over a Stage-coach pofition'd on the pavement beneath, killing the unfortunate Creature, & breaking his own Leg, but hobbling away from his Triumph with handfome winnings of £12,000.

He has lately compleated an aftounding Endeavour which we feel certain will bring him lafting Fame. At a Dinner given laft Year by His Grace the DUKE of LEINSTER, it was agreed that Mr. Whaley fhould attempt to walk to *Jerufalem,* play Hand-ball againft the celebrated *Wailing Wall* in that City, & walk back to *Ireland,* all within the compafs of a Twelve-month.

Mr. Whaley departed *Dublin* in the company of an impartial Obferver on the 29th of *September* laft Year, difcharg'd his fporting Duty in *Jerufalem,* & return'd this Month to celebratory Bonfires on his native foil, & an enviable Purfe of £15,000. His matchlefs Exploit is commemorated in a Song entitl'd *Round the World for Sport,* & he is now known to his Friends as *Jerufalem Whaley.*

Of itſelf, Age need not be any great Obſtacle to continuing Succeſs, yet the diſilluſionment & Ennui that can dog a Man in his advancing Years will lead him to queſtion whether he ſtill has the ſtomach for the Struggle. It would have been obvious, even to thoſe of baſe & witleſs Capacity, that the Dawn of my Fifth Decade as an Editor found my Spirits greatly jaded, & I fix'd an Eye firmly upon the means of making the remaining Time allotted to me in this World as comfortable & as tranquil as Circumſtances would allow.

On infrequent viſits to my houſe in *Clerkenwell,* my dear Siſter, Mrs. GERTRUDE STROAKER, oft remark'd upon my growing Averſion to my fellow Man. It ſeem'd to Her that my many Years of cataloguing & commentating upon the moral Lapſes of our Betters had taken its toll upon my Conſtitution & general Happyneſs, & I ſuppoſe the Gravamen of her obſervation was found.

Decrepitude & Gout had not entirely engulf'd me, but I was not the youthful figure who had ſought to make his mark upon the World Forty Years before. A Rheum would often cloud my eyes, & a perſiſtent infirmity of the Bladder was not in any wiſe remedy'd by a preſcrib'd courſe of Palliatives & Tinctures. Taking the waters at the Iſlington Spa only ſerv'd to increaſe the already copious Volume & frequency of Micturition that dogg'd my waking Hours, & wrench'd me nightly from the arms of *Morpheus.* As a conſequence, Mr. Stroaker began to take on thoſe Duties which included the cuſtomary Three-bottle Dinner with looſe-tongu'd informants at my Club, tho' I'll warrant he did not ſee this as any great Hardſhip. Shepherding the errant Mr. Jakes from the Gin-ſhops & *Bagnios* to his copper Plates likewiſe became a Taſk I was happy to relinquiſh into the hands of my ſpirited Nephew.

It muſt be obſerv'd that at this time Mr. Jakes did ſurpriſe us all with a ſudden Ebullition of fervent Patriotiſm. As the Revolution in *France* took on an ever more horrific aſpect, he ſought to contraſt ſteadfaſt *Engliſh* Loyalty & Duty with *Gallick* Barbarity by means of Caricatures guying the ſavagery of the *Sans-Culottes.* When the Deſpotiſm & Demagoguery of the upſtart BONAPARTE began to caſt a dark ſhadow over *Britannia's* domeſtick & foreign intereſts, Mr. Jakes turn'd his ſatirickal Artillery on the bold *Corſican,* with many admir'd reſults. Whenever news of one of our martial Victories gain'd common Currency, a tear of Pride would ſpring to the old rogue's remaining eye. I was ſtruck forcibly by a fondneſs & Admiration for him I never previouſly credited poſſible.

While Perfidy & Revolution rag'd uncheck'd in *France,* news had reach'd our ſhores of a MUTINY in the South Seas by a young Officer aboard one of His Majeſty's ſhips, & a ſtrong appetite for further Intelligence of this event was engender'd in our Readerſhip. ————

OF THE MUTINOUS SEIZURE
& THE DOGGED LT. BLIGH'S SUBSEQUENT

The BREADFRUIT
Artocarpus altilis

Lt. WILLIAM BLIGH R.N. is pleaſ'd to announce the Publication of his *Narrative of the MUTINY on Board His Majeſty's Ship the* BOUNTY. In this ſingular Work he gives affecting Accounts of both the heinous Seizure of that Veſſel by its Acting Lieutenant, Mr. FLETCHER CHRISTIAN, & the ſtout-hearted Exploit of his ſailing the Ship's loyal Men in an Open-boat a diſtance of 3,618 nautickal Miles, to the ſafe-haven of *Coupang*, in the *Dutch* dominion of *Timor*.

The *Bounty* was captain'd by Mr. Bligh under the Patronage of Sir JOSEPH BANKS, & ſhe ſail'd from *Spithead* in *December* of 1787, her Commander being charg'd with the Duty of procuring Bread-fruit trees from the Natives of the Iſland of *Otaheite* in the *South-ſeas*, & carrying them to the *Weſt Indies*, where they were to be cultivated as Food for the Slaves on our Sugar-plantations. Having ſojourn'd upwards of Five Months with the beguiling *Otaheitians*, the Bounty's courſe was ſet for her Paſſage to the *Weſt Indies*, while replete with her ſizeable Cargo of 1,015 Plants. On the 28th of *April* laſt Year, an unaccountable *Animus* towards Mr. Bligh on Mr. Chriſtian's part led to an infamous Mutiny by the young Maſter's Mate & a Company of pliant Con-federates, which was expedited, in Mr. Bligh's Opinion, by the effects upon the Crew of the Allurements of venereal Diſſipation at *Otaheite*. Mr. Bligh & his loyal Adherents were ſet adrift in the Ship's Open-boat, which was but 23ft. in length, & they were ſupply'd by Mr. Chriſtian with little more than a few Charts, a Quadrant, & Victuals barely ſufficient to ſuſtain the 18 Men for a ſpan of One Week. Tho' the unhappy Party ſuffer'd harrowing Privations of foul Weather, Thirſt, & Starvation, but one Man was loſt on the Voyage of 43 Days, when his Brains were beaten out by the Savages of *Tofoa*, the Boat's only landfall. The Deliverance of the remainder of the Men is attributed to Mr. Bligh's matchleſs Seamanſhip & Reſolution.

Mr. Bligh return'd to *England* in *March* of this Year, & the Court Martial he ſhall face as a conſequence of the loſs of his Ship ſhall doubtleſs prove little more than a Formality, blameleſs as his Actions muſt be adjudg'd in this caſe. It is likewiſe probable that he ſhall be diſpatch'd to *Otaheite* in another Ship by the Admiralty, to compleat a taſk thwarted by Rebellion & Villainy.

Looks like Burkitt's trying to nail another One...

OF H.M.S. *BOUNTY*, PRECIPITATED BY MISLAY'D COCOA-NUTS, OPEN-BOAT NAVIGATION.

OF THE CHARACTER OF MR. CHRISTIAN.

THE Fate of the Mutineers is a matter of Conjecture, tho' Mr. Bligh believes that it was surely their Intention to resume their voluptuous Lives at *Otaheite*, where, for the Fee of an Iron Nail, the Favours of the comely Women might be bought by lascivious *British* Tars. His Majesty's Royal Navy will doubtless mount an Expedition to hunt down the Malefactors, & Mr. Bligh's short Accounts of their physickal Characters, & the Tattoos they got at the hands of the *Otaheitians*, will prove invaluable in this Endeavour. He describes Mr. Christian thus :-

The COCOA-NUT
Cocos nucifera

5 Ft., 9 In. High. Blackish *or very dark brown* Complexion. Dark Brown Hair. Strong made. A Star tatowed on his left Breast and tatowed on the backside. His knees stand a little out and he may be called a little Bowlegged. He is subject to Violent perspiration, particularly in his hands so that he Soils anything he handles.

Mr. Christian is of a respectable Family of *Cumberland* & the *Isle of Man*, & his treacherous Action will greatly surprise his Relations. He had been on very good Terms with Mr. Bligh, having sail'd with him on Three previous Occasions, but it would seem that he felt very keenly the many Chastisements & Complaints of the *Bounty's* assiduous Commander as slights upon his Honour.

When he was accus'd by Mr. Bligh of pilfering from his private store of Cocoa-nuts aboard *Bounty*, Mr. Christian was mortify'd beyond description, & it would seem that at this Juncture he resolv'd to brook no further Insults. Having been persuaded by one of the Midshipman not to abandon the Ship on a ramshackle Raft, & that the Men were ripe for anything, he resolv'd to wrest the Bounty from Mr. Bligh.

On the Morning of the Mutiny, when he had been awoken at the point of a Cutlass by Mr. Christian, & his hands tied, Mr. Bligh sought to remind the young Officer of the many Instances of Kindness he had shewn him. This seem'd to affect Mr. Christian markedly, & perhaps stung by the acute Awareness of the Obligation he had been made to feel by Mr. Bligh, he reply'd in a most agitated manner, *That, Captain Bligh – that is the thing ! I am in HELL ! I am in HELL !* He at least demonstrated that he had sufficient mastery over his Passions to prevent his fellow Mutineers acting upon their Threats, directed at Mr. Bligh, that they would *Shoot the Bugger !*

Mr. Bligh's preferr'd Remedy for Laxity is to lash his Subordinates with his Tongue, rather than the Cat-o'-Nine-Tails, & we feel his new Sobriquet of the *Bounty Bastard* is a vile calumny on his Character.

OF A NEW THEATRICKAL PRESENTATION OF THE BOUNTY's MUTINY.

THE *Royalty Theatre*, on *Well-street*, now presents every Evening a Performance of *THE PIRATES, Or The Calamities of Capt. BLIGH*, being a full Account of his Voyage, & shewing the *Bounty* sailing down the *River Thames* ; Mr. Bligh's Reception at *Otaheite*, & the Exchange of *British* Goods for Bread-fruit ; with an *Otaheitian* Dance ; an exact Representation of the Seizure of Mr. Bligh in the Cabin of the Ship by the Pirates ; his being forc'd with his faithful followers into the Boat, & their Distress at sea ; their subsequent arrival at the *Cape of Good Hope* ; the Dances & Ceremonies of the *Hottentots* on their Departure ; & their happy return to *England* ; the whole being stag'd under the direct Instruction of a person who was aboard the *Bounty*.

The Part of Mr. Bligh is taken by the Theatre's Proprietor, Mr. RALPH WEWITZER, & the Part of Mr. Christian is taken by Mr. WILLIAM BOURKE.

The Gin-Lane Gazette

PUBLISHED in LONDON — December, 1790. — Nathaniel Crowquill Efq.

PARTICULARS CONCERNING Mr. RENWICK WILLIAMS, FOUND GUILTY OF THE MALICIOUS CRIMES OF THE KNIFE-WIELDING MONSTER.

IT is a matter of Conjecture whether the Conviction & Imprifonment of Mr. RENWICK WILLIAMS for numerous violent Crimes, perpetrated againft feveral Ladies of *London*, will quell the Fears of a phrenzy'd Publick, given the many doubts lately articulated concerning the Reliability of the Verdict, return'd on the 14th of *December* at his Third Trial.

The Affaults, upon upwards of Fifty Ladies, were begun in May of the Year 1788 by a Man who follow'd his Victims, ranted remarks of a lewd Nature at them, & ftabb'd them in the Thighs or Buttocks with a fmall Knife. It was often reported that he alfo had Blades faften'd to his Knees. A general Panick enfu'd, during which arm'd Protectors roam'd the ftreets of the City, Ladies took to wearing Cooking-coppers againft their rumps to guard them from Blades, & a Company of Gentlemen eftablifh'd a *No Monfter Club*, & fported Emblems upon their Coats to fignify that they were not the Felon, who was dubb'd The MONSTER by fome Gentlemen of the Prefs. A Performance entitl'd *The MONSTER, Or, The Wounded Ladies*, was put on at Mr. Aftley's Theatre, & enjoy'd great Popularity.

The *Bow-ftreet* Conftables were hinder'd in their Efforts to apprehend the Fiend by the manifold Defcriptions of him with which they were fupply'd, no Two Accounts of his Appearance being the fame. Mr. JOHN JULIUS ANGERSTEIN was pleaf'd to offer a Reward of £100 for the Capture of the Affailant, with the unhappy Confequence that countlefs arrefts of blamelefs Men were made by zealous & fpeculative Citizens.

In the midft of this ungovernable Clamour & Confufion, Mr. RENWICK WILLIAMS was taken by the Conftables on the 13th of *June* this Year, with the affiftance of Mr. JOHN COLEMAN, an Admirer of one ANN PORTER, who had been attack'd on the 18th of *January* laft. Mr. Williams was identify'd as the Monfter by that Lady, yet he maintain'd that he was innocent of the Charge, which after much Deliberation was lay'd againft him as one of Affault, of Mifs Porter & his fundry other Victims. His Firft Trial was held at the *Seffions Houfe* of the *Old Bailey* on the 8th of *July*, during which many Witneffes affirm'd that the Accuf'd had been at his Work at the time of the alleg'd Attack upon Mifs Porter's perfon. Notwithftanding thefe & other favourable Characters, & the Doubts voic'd by Mr. Angerftein concerning his Culpability, Mr. Williams was found Guilty. However, the Judge prefiding prov'd reluctant to fentence Mr. Williams, & expreff'd Refervations concerning the Evidence given againft him. He therefore referr'd the cafe to *High Courts*, which overturn'd the Conviction on a nicety of the law, but the Offence was nonethelefs deem'd a High Mifdemeanour. A Retrial was order'd as a Confequence, after the Thirteen Hours' duration of which Mr. Williams was found Guilty, & fentenc'd to a Term of Six Years' Imprifonment at *Newgate*.

Mr. Williams is a former Lawyer's Clerk, who had been employ'd as an Artificial-flower Maker in *Dover-ftreet*, before his Indictment. He is often call'd upon in his Cell at *Newgate* by curious Vifitors, to whom he fells his Flowers, having refum'd his Trade within that Gaol's formidable Walls.

PARTICULARS CONCERNING THE PRINCE OF WALES'S HORSE, ESCAPE, & SUSPICIONS OF ROYAL DUPLICITY ON THE TURF.

ALLEGATIONS of difhonourable Dealing have been levell'd by the Stewards of *Newmarket* at His Royal Highnefs, the PRINCE of WALES, & Mr. SAM CHIFNEY, his Jockey, concerning the outcomes of Two Races run at that Ground by the Prince's Horfe, ESCAPE.

On the 20th of *October,* Mr. Chifney rode Efcape as the Favourite in a Race of Two Miles, at odds of 1–2 for a 60-Guinea Purfe, but the Horfe finifh'd laft behind Coriander, Skylark, & Pipator. The Day following, both His Royal Highnefs & Mr. Chifney lay'd Bets on Efcape – his odds upon that Occafion being lengthen'd to 5–1 in the light of his poor fhewing in the previous Race – & he went on to enjoy a decifive Victory over Chanticleer, Skylark, Grey Diomed, Harpator, & Alderman, fecuring the Purfe of 60 Guineas for the Prince. There follow'd directly vociferous Proteftations that His Highnefs had inftructed Mr. Chifney to fpoil Efcape in the Firft Race, that they might both profit handfomely by his unexpected Succefs in the Second. The Prince damn'd thefe Charges as Calumnies & rafcally Lies, & difpatch'd his

Come, Chifney — We're leaving!

Friend, Mr. RICHARD BRINSLEY SHERIDAN, to arbitrate at *Newmarket* on his behalf, but Sir CHARLES BUNBURY & other Gentlemen of the *Jockey Club* felt compell'd to enquire more clofely into the matter.

Mr. Chifney was queftion'd, & fwore that he had not in any wife hinder'd Efcape's progrefs in the Firft Race, but Sir Charles & his Confederates were not perfuaded that no Deception had taken place. Sir Charles has lately advif'd His Royal Highnefs that if Mr. Chifney were permitted to ride the Prince's Horfes upon future Occafions, no Gentleman would race againft him. The Prince has taken this Admonifhment very ill, has vow'd that he fhall no longer favour *Newmarket* with his Prefence, & is pondering the Termination of all his dealings with the Turf. He remains entirely fatisfy'd that Mr. Chifney conducted himfelf honourably in the Affair, & is pleaf'd to continue affording him his Salary of £200 *per annum,* for Life.

Printed for the PROPRIETOR by A. CULLY, at the *Strutting Cock,*
In *St. Paul's Churchyard,* where Advertifements, & Letters to the Editor, are taken in.

AN ACCOUNT OF THE VOLCANO AT RANELAGH GARDENS.

THE Managers at RANELAGH GARDENS lately aftound their patrons with an authentick and tumultuous volcanick difplay, to rival the prefent and continuous eruptions at the true Mount AETNA, obferved by a tremulous *Italian* populace fince the 23rd day of laft month.

This fingular and celebrated exhibition, which meets with univerfal acclaim, was firft given in the year 1772 at *Marylebone Gardens* for the KING's Birthday, by Signor GIOVANNI BATTISTA TORRÉ. During the performance, a curtain rifes to reveal the *Forge of Vulcan,* fhewing that god and the *Cyclops* forging the armour of *Mars* on the flopes of *Mount Aetna,* and *Venus* entreating them to fafhion arrows for *Cupid,* her fon. The forge then belches forth thick fmoak, the mountain's crater vomits flames, and lava pours down the eminence with encreafing ferocity, until the finale of a mighty eruption, the whole being accompanied by the mufick of Meffrs. Haydn, Handel, Gluck, and Giardini. It is thought that the fiery effects, under the direction of Mr. THOMAS BROCK, are produced by the expedient of attaching rockets to guiding ropes, and troughs of water lit from beneath counterfeit the mountain's rivers of lava moft fuccefsfully.

In the year 1770, Signor Torré had the honour of directing the fireworks at the marriage of King LOUIS XVI and Queen MARIE ANTOINETTE, and did likewife for an entertainment given in the year 1774 by the late Mr. DAVID GARRICK. Upon one occafion, Signor Torré expofed his myftickal inclinations to Mr. Garrick, and offer'd to furnifh him with inftructions for the harvefting of Celeftial Manna, and to reveal the fecrets of the *Cabbala.*

OBITUARY:
LORD HELLGATE BARRYMORE,
DIED 6TH OF MARCH, 1793.

WE regret that it is our fad Duty to inform our Readers of the untimely paffing of a Friend to His Royal Highnefs the PRINCE of WALES, an *Old Etonian,* a Frequenter of the Turf & the Bawdy-houfes, & one thought of by all as a riotous fon of Intemperance, Richard Barry, Seventh EARL of BARRYMORE.

Lord Barrymore inherited his deceaf'd Father's Eftate of 140,000 acres, in *County Cork, Ireland,* a fhort while before his Fourth Birth-day. In his Youth, he was allow'd by all to be well-read, could be moft engaging Company, & became an accomplifh'd Actor, Jockey, Pugilift, Cricketer, & Fencer. Yet for all his admirable Qualities, he frequently difplay'd an exafperating fide to his Character. As an Adherent of the *Botherers' Club,* he was a notorious practitioner of Japery, & would place Coffins outfide the Houfes of refpectable Perfons to frighten their Servants, & was known to abduct young Ladies from the Streets of *London.* No Man was more enflav'd to a fpeculative Nature, & for a Wager he once rode his Horfe to the higheft Floor of the Home of Mrs. FITZHERBERT, the *Inamorata* of the Prince of Wales. Two Blackfmiths were later fummon'd to pufh the Horfe back down the Staircafe, when it refuf'd to extricate itfelf. Lord Barrymore alfo accepted a challenge to eat a live Cat in One Sitting, but baulk'd at the Tafk at the laft moment. His taftes prov'd more exotick when he ferv'd a Turtle weighing 150lbs., at an Election Dinner in *Reading.*

Unfurprifingly, his unwarrantable Behaviour won him many Enemies, & he retain'd the Services of the Prize-fighter, BILLY The Tin-man HOOPER, as his Bully & Protector.

Lord Barrymore once won a Purfe of £25,000 on a conteft between Mr. Hooper & Mr. Bob Watfon, & the former inftructed him in the Pugilift's Art.

In the Year 1788, Lord Barrymore built a private Theatre at *Wargrave,* his Eftate, at a coft of £60,000. Not content with this, he alfo purchaf'd Squib's Auction-rooms in *Savile-row,* & had them converted into a Theatre, performing often upon its Stage himfelf. He accru'd fizeable Debts on this Venture, however, & the Theatre & its contents were foon feiz'd & fold off.

In *June* of laft Year, he fold his Family's Eftates, & elop'd to much publick Condemnation with the Daughter of a Sedan Chair-man, whom he marry'd, but his connubial Joy was to prove tranfient. He had join'd the *Berkfhire Militia* as an Enfign, & on the 6th Day of this Month, was entrufted with the Duty of efcorting fome *French* Prifoners through the County of *Kent.* After taking Victuals at an Inn near *Folkeftone,* Lord Barrymore difcharg'd his Firearm by accident while mounting his Gig, & fhot himfelf through the Eye. He clung to Life for a mere Forty Minutes thereafter, the rofeate bloom of Youth ftill upon him, being but Twenty-four Years old. Rumours abound that he was bury'd in fecret, to prevent his Creditors from requifitioning his Corpfe until his confiderable Debts were fettl'd.

Well met, Lad!

Known to his Intimates by the Cognomen *Hellgate,* owing to his devilifh Mifdemeanours, Lord Barrymore's Demife will be mourn'd by his Siblings, who are likewife known by fimilarly pejorative Sobriquets. Lord Barrymore's Brother, a wenching Gamefter & debt-ridden Clergyman, is known to all as *Newgate,* as it is confidently predicted he will one Day find himfelf in Gaol. Another Brother, to whom the Earldom fhall pafs, is burden'd with a Club-foot, & is known as *Cripplegate,* & his Sifter CAROLINE, Lady MELFORT, is known as *Billingfgate,* fince fhe is as foul-mouth'd as any Fifh-wife of *Billingfgate* Market.

OF THE DEATH OF LT. HUGH MUNRO, KILL'D BY A TIGER IN BENGAL.

THE Perils of Life in our *Indian* Dominions have been fhewn to be always near at hand, not only by the lamentable Death of Lt. HUGH MUNRO, who died of Wounds he fuftain'd when he fuffer'd a dreadful Attack by a TIGER, but by the troubling relifh with which this Calamity is greeted by the belligerent SULTAN of MYSORE.

Lt. Munro was fojourning with a Party of Friends on *Saugur Ifland,* in *Weft Bengal,* in *December* of laft Year. The Company had broken off from Hunting to partake of Victuals, when Lt. Munro was fet upon by a cruel & immenfe royal Tiger, reported to have been 4½ Ft. high, & 9 Ft. long, which carry'd him off into the Vegetation. Lt. Munro was refcu'd by his Friends, but expir'd of his terrible Wounds the Day following.

This Misfortune has come to the attention of the Demagogue TIPPOO SAIB, the Sultan of *Myfore,* who has rul'd his mountainous Province fince the Year 1782, & who has made a Cult of the Tiger as a mark of his Ferocity, bedecking his Palace at *Seringapatam,* & his Throne, Cannon, & Swords, with renderings of that terrible Beaft. In Celebration of Lt. Munro's Demife, Tippoo order'd a colourful Sculpture to be made, of a fize authentick to Life, of the Tiger favaging a proftrate *Britifh* Soldier, & from infide of which a mechanickal Organ emits the found of the Creature's Growling, & the Shrieks of its unfortunate Victim.

We underftand that the Potteries of *Staffordfhire* will foon offer to their Patrons a fmaller, earthenware Figure of Lt. Munro & the Tiger, to commemorate this awful Mifadventure.

VAUXHALL, AUGUST 27TH, 1793. - On this Day THE GARDENS will CLOSE for this Seafon. In addition to the ufual Entertainments, His Royal Highnefs the DUKE of YORK's Band (by permiffion in full Uniform) will perform between the Acts, & conclude the Evening with feveral favourite pieces of MARTIAL MUSIC. The Gardens will be illuminated with great BRILLIANCY. Admittance Two Shillings.

DUKE of YORK

WE PRESENT TO OUR READERS OUR BOLD BEAUTY FOR THE MONTH OF OCTOBER, LADY HAMILTON.

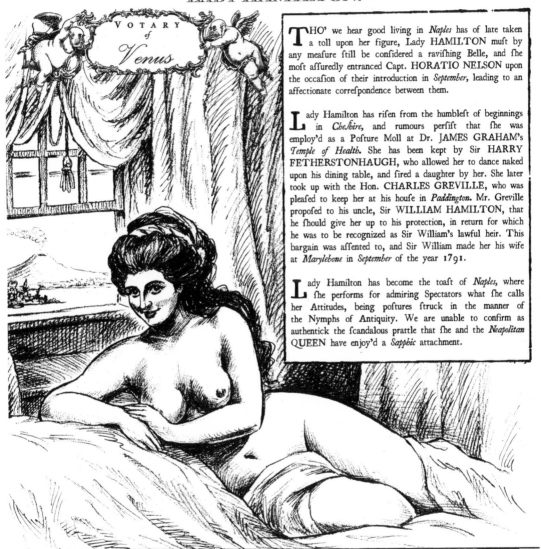

VOTARY *of* Venus

THO' we hear good living in *Naples* has of late taken a toll upon her figure, Lady HAMILTON muſt by any meaſure ſtill be conſidered a raviſhing Belle, and ſhe moſt aſſuredly entranced Capt. HORATIO NELSON upon the occaſion of their introduction in *September,* leading to an affectionate correſpondence between them.

Lady Hamilton has riſen from the humbleſt of beginnings in *Cheſhire,* and rumours perſiſt that ſhe was employ'd as a Poſture Moll at Dr. JAMES GRAHAM's *Temple of Health.* She has been kept by Sir HARRY FETHERSTONHAUGH, who allowed her to dance naked upon his dining table, and ſired a daughter by her. She later took up with the Hon. CHARLES GREVILLE, who was pleaſed to keep her at his houſe in *Paddington.* Mr. Greville propoſed to his uncle, Sir WILLIAM HAMILTON, that he ſhould give her up to his protection, in return for which he was to be recognized as Sir William's lawful heir. This bargain was aſſented to, and Sir William made her his wife at *Marylebone* in *September* of the year 1791.

Lady Hamilton has become the toaſt of *Naples,* where ſhe performs for admiring Spectators what ſhe calls her Attitudes, being poſtures ſtruck in the manner of the Nymphs of Antiquity. We are unable to confirm as authentick the ſcandalous prattle that ſhe and the *Neapolitan* QUEEN have enjoy'd a *Sapphic* attachment.

THE SURGEON & ANATOMIST, Dr. JOHN HUNTER, having departed this Life on the 16th of OCTO-BER, bequeath'd to the Nation his Collection of anatomickal Curioſities, amongſt which is the Skeleton of CHARLES BYRNE, known as the ſurpriſing IRISH GIANT. In Life, Mr. Byrne was around 8 Ft. tall, & was exhibited at Mr. Wigley's Umbrella Shop, *Spring-garden Gate,* next door to *Cox's Muſeum.* He was an immoderate drinker, & fell into Melancholy when his Life's fortune of £700 was ſtolen from him. He died at *Charing-croſs* in the Year 1783, at the Age of Twenty-Two. Fearing that the Anatomiſts would diſſect him for chirurgickal Scrutiny, he had requeſted to be bury'd at Sea, but the late Dr. Hunter brib'd his Undertaker with the ſum of £500, & had his Corpſe appropriated.

OF THE LATE MR. EDWARD GIBBON's EGREGIOUSLY SWOLLEN TESTICLES.

THE eſtimable author of *The HISTORY of the DECLINE and FALL of the ROMAN EMPIRE*, Mr. EDWARD GIBBON, has ſuffered a death as rare as any diſſolute Ancient, having expir'd as a conſequence of complications ariſing from ſurgery upon his vaſt Teſticles.

Upon hearing of the demiſe of the wife of Lord SHEFFIELD, Mr. Gibbon returned without delay to *England* from his houſe at *Lake Geneva,* in order to offer ſolace to his bereaved friend, and was forced to traverſe the war-torn expanſe of *Europe* to do ſo. He had ſuſtained a Rupture in his groin while ſerving with the military many years ago, and the ſac this injury engendered became turgid with fluids. Having once dropt to his knees to aſk for Lady ELIZABETH FOSTER's hand in marriage, he endured the indignity of having to be helped to his feet by ſervants, ſo cumberſome was his fleſhy burden. Of late, the protuberance had ſwollen ſo greatly as to become almoſt as big as a ſmall child, tho' he fondly imagined that it was never noticed by others.

It was decided that the only remedy was to tap the ſac, and draw off its contents, which Mr. Gibbon ſubmitted to with ſingular chearfulneſs, regaling his ſurgeon with the following politickal jeſt as he was buſy with the knife : *Why is a fat man like a Corniſh Borough? Becauſe he never ſees his member.* Mr. Gibbon underwent three ſuch procedures, but a few days after the laſt of theſe, a terrible infection broke out in the wound, and corrupted his blood, and he departed this life on the 16th of *January.* He is interred at *Fletching,* in the County of *Suſſex.*

Do your worſt, Sir!

I admire your Balls.

WONDER OF WONDERS ! ! !

THE Nobility, Gentry, &c. are hereby informed, they may have an ocular demonſtration of a natural and true MERMAID, juſt arrived, an amazing creature, moſt rare, remarkably curious for its aſtoniſhing ſtructure, and the only one of its kind ever ſeen in *Europe* ſince the Archduke of *Auſtria's,* which is upwards of 245 years ago.

This wonderful *Nymph of the Sea,* half woman from the head down to the lower part of the waiſt, and half fiſh from thence downwards, is three feet long, having ears, gills, breaſts, fins, ſhoulders, arms, hands, fingers, and a contiguous ſcale covering only the fiſh part ; and is allowed by all thoſe who have ſeen it to be the moſt extraordinary fiſh ever ſeen in the world. It is exhibited from Ten in the morning till duſk,

AT

Mr. Elliot's, Carpenter, No.7, in *Broad-court, Bow-ſtreet, Covent-garden.* Admittance One Shilling each perſon.

The SEVEN DIALS STROLLER

PARTICULARS CONCERNING THE SUBLIME SOCIETY OF BEEF-STEAKS, & THE MALODOROUS DUKE OF NORFOLK'S INSATIABLE APPETITE.

Eſtabliſh'd as it was in the Year 1735 in proteſt at the Fripperies of *French* Cuiſine, the SUBLIME SOCIETY of BEEF-STEAKS has welcom'd ſuch illuſtrious Members at the late Mr. WILLIAM HOGARTH, the late Mr. DAVID GARRICK, Mr. JOHN WILKES, Mr. CHARLES JAMES FOX, the late EARL of SANDWICH, the DUKE of YORK, and His Royal Highneſs The PRINCE of WALES, but in the corpulent figure of His Grace the DUKE of NORFOLK, it now boaſts its moſt dedicated Devotee of honeſt *Britiſh* Fayre ſince its foundation.

The Duke begins an Evening's Dining at a Tavern with a ſupper of Fiſh, before proceeding to the Society's room at the *Covent-garden* Theatre, where ſweaty Hirelings at an open fire ſear Beef-ſteaks on a Grid-iron – a rendering of which might alſo be ſeen upon the braſs Buttons of the Members' Coats – which are thereafter ſerv'd to the Diners without delay. The Duke thinks nothing of devouring at One Sitting a remarkable Three Helpings, perhaps amounting to Four Pounds of Beef, and he is rumour'd to have outdone himſelf upon one occaſion by conſuming an aſtoniſhing Fifteen Steaks. He will afterwards chop Beet-root, and a Spaniſh Onion, combine them with Oil and Vinegar, and cleanſe his Palate with this Concoction. The other Members will likewiſe round off their Repaſts with toaſted Cheeſe, Punch, Porter, Whiſky-toddies, and a Pipe or two of Tobacco. It is the Taſk of the Society's Preſident to ſing the Song of the Day, and the Members compoſe their own Muſick for certain Occaſions.

The Duke of Norfolk is condemn'd as a *vulgar, heavy, clumſy, dirty-looking Maſs of Matter*, who has enjoy'd *libidinous Amours without Delicacy, and without number,*

diſplaying the *intemperate indulgence of animal Impulſe.* He has a Capacity for Liquor as great as his Appetite for Victuals, and drinks intemperately until he becomes entirely inſenſible in his Chair, whereupon a Servant rings for Four Footmen bearing a Stretcher, who lay His Grace upon it with a Dexterity betraying long Practiſe, and carry him to his Bed-chamber. Since he is habitually filthy in his Perſon, and rarely makes uſe of Water, the Servants often take advantage of his inebriated Condition to remove his Cloaths, and ſcrub his bloated Carcaſs with Soap and Water.

OF MRS. SALMON'S WAX-WORKS.

Mrs. SALMON's celebrated Eſtabliſhment at No. 189, *Fleet-ſtreet* offers to its Patrons a moſt diverting Exhibition of Wax-works, being prodigiouſly Life-like Effigies of 140 Human Figures, amongſt which are Kings & Queens, Merlin, & an ancient Woman fleeing from the figure of Time with his Hour-glaſs, who ſhakes his ſnowy Head with ſorrow at ſeeing Age ſo unwilling to die. An amuſing Automaton in the Character of the Witch & Propheteſs, OLD MOTHER SHIPTON, ſupports herſelf with Crutches, & kicks the Arſes of Viſitors as they leave the Premiſes.

OF THE PRIZE-FIGHT WON BY MRS. MARY ANN FIELDING.

SATURDAY, 5th of JUNE - The celebrated Heroes of the Fancy, Mr. JOHN *Gentleman* JACKSON & Mr. DANIEL MENDOZA, were pleas'd to act as Seconds in a pugiliſtick Conteſt, fought by one MARY ANN FIELDING, & a JEWESS of *Wentworth-ſtreet.*

The Match, for Two Guineas a-ſide, took place near the *New Road* in *London,* & Two of the Women's own Sex were their Bottle-holders. Mrs. Fielding gave a well-conducted Diſplay of the noble Art of Boxing, & beſted her Opponent in One Hour & Twenty Minutes, knocking the Jeweſs down on around Seventy Occaſions.

On the 15th of *April,* Mr. Jackſon was declar'd the Champion of all *England* in a Match of Ten & a Half Minutes' duration againſt Mr. Mendoza, at *Hornchurch,* in the County of *Eſſex.* Mr. Jackſon's Victory was diſputed due to his graſping Mr. Mendoza's Hair & beating him until he was render'd incapable, but this *modus operandi* was at length deem'd fair.

AN ACCOUNT OF THE HIGHWAYMAN, JERRY ABERSHAW, WHO FAC'D DEATH WITH NOT A LITTLE PANACHE.

3rd of AUGUST - AFTER a felonious Career of Five Years' duration, the Highwayman & Scoundrel, JERRY ABERSHAW – One amongst a dwindling Breed of mounted Ruffians – was turned off upon the Gallows, tho' not before difplaying proud Infolence & carelefs Effrontery at the Profpect of his own Demife.

Aberfhaw & his affociate, *Galloping* Dick FERGUSON, were members of an infamous Gang, who perpetrated their vile Crimes upon *Wimbledon Common* & *Putney Heath*, & whofe favour'd Tavern was the *Bald-Fac'd Stag Inn*, near *Kingfton*. Aberfhaw fhot Two *Bow-ftreet* Runners during his arreft at the *Three Brewers* Ale-houfe in *Southwark*, & when convicted upon the evidence of the furviving Officer, he mock'd the Court by placing his Hat upon his Head as the Judge donn'd the black Cap which prefages the Death Sentence. While awaiting Execution, Aberfhaw requefted that black Cherries be fent to his Gaol-cell, & uf'd their juice to draw pictures of his contemptible Exploits on the Walls.

He was taken in jocular Spirits to the Gallows at *Kennington Common*, & afcended the Ladder with a Rofe between his Teeth. He then threw to the Mob a Prayer-book that had been offer'd to him, before kicking off his Shoes, as he wifh'd to difprove his Mother's Prediction that he would die with his Boots on. He was allow'd to be a good-looking Rafcal, & is thought to have been Twenty-two Years of Age.

The place at *Putney* where his Body is now gibbeted is lately become known as *Jerry's Hill.*

TO THE EDITOR:

SIR ——

WHILE this Nation has in the perfon of Mr. WILLIAM PITT the youngeft Prime Minifter ever to hold that auguft office, it moft affuredly now boafts its THIRSTIEST alfo. I have difcovered that his appetite for liquor was engendered in his youth by a Doctor, who prefcribed a bottle of Port a day to aid his conftitution. Taking this advice to heart, and perhaps cultivating the opinion that while a little is good, a great deal must be confiderably better, Mr. Pitt is now known to imbibe in excefs of three bottles of Port Wine a day !

He has upon occafion fo befuddled himfelf in drink – in the company of his friend, Mr. DUNDAS – that he has been obliged to poftpone replies to his opponents in the *Houfe of Commons,* and frequently quaffs himfelf into infenfibility at the *Tory* Balls of Her Grace the DUCHESS of GORDON.

Ah, Your Grace — permit me to introduce my new Chancellor of the Exchequer!

Yet if he is intemperate in his drinking, we muft allow that he is abftemious in carnal purfuits, and maintains his bachelordom with the affiduity of a Cardinal. I am reminded of thofe fatirickal lines in *The Rolliad,* which jibed at his celibacy with not a little ribaldry :

> 'Tis true, indeed, we oft abufe him,
> Becaufe he bends to no man ;
> But Slander's felf dares not accufe him
> Of Stiffnefs to a woman.

I have the Honour to remain,
Yours, &c.
M.B., St. James's.

PIDCOCK's
Grand MENAGERIE of Foreign Animals & Birds,

Over *Exeter-'Change, Strand, London,*
and feen in Market-Places in fundry Towns,
drawn by Twenty Horfes, in Four magnificent Caravans,

WHICH was pleafed to fhow four Years hence the DOUBLE-HEADED COW, which took fuftenance with both Mouths at the fame time, and was infpected and admired by the late JOHN HUNTER, Profeffor of Anatomy, now invites the Publick to an Exhibition of the

REAL UNICORN, or Rhinoceros,

Being at leaft twelve feet long, and the Circumference of its Body being nearly equal to its Length ; though not above two Years of age, the Expenfe of his Food and Journey amounted to near one thoufand pounds fterling. He is fo gentle, that any Perfon may approach him with the greateft Safety.

Also a moft ftupendous MALE ELEPHANT,

The largeft ever feen in *Great Britain.* The Sagacity and Knowledge of this extraordinary Animal is abfolutely beyond Human Imagination ; it will lie down and rife up at a Word of Command, notwithftanding the many Tales that are told of their having no Joints in their Legs ; it will take up the fmalleft piece of Money, a Tankard, a Bucket, or anything elfe, and deliver it to any Perfon in the Company.

Alfo a beautiful ZEBRA ;

It is remarkably ftriped, and is quite another variety to that which our Queen had prefented to her about thirty Years back. The works of the Creator are wonderfully difplayed in the fine Features and Elegance of this remarkable Animal.

Alfo a fine young LION ;

This moft magnificent Animal is fuperior in Courage, and univerfally acknowledged the fole Monarch of the Whole of Brute Creation, ftriking Terror throughout the Kingdom of Quadrupeds, and attaining a prodigious Strength and Ferocity.

Alfo Two *Royal Bengal* TIGERS ; Two beautiful fpotted LEOPARDS ; A HYAENA, which imitates the Human voice in a very ftriking manner ; An ANTELOPE, faid to be the *fwifteft* Animal on the Face of the Globe ; and a *South American* VULTURE, or Condor Minor, from the *Brazils.*

Roll up! Roll up!

Admittance – One Shilling each.

N.B. Foreign Beafts & Birds bought, fold, or exchanged, by G. PIDCOCK ; enquire as above.

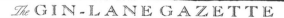

PARTICULARS OF THE WAGER AT BRIGHTON OF SIR JOHN LADE & LORD CHOLMONDELEY, ENTAILING THE NAKEDNESS OF THE LATTER.

LAST month, a Wager for a trifling Sum was agreed between Sir JOHN LADE & Lord CHOLMONDELEY, on the bafis of an Affertion by Sir John that he could carry His Lordfhip twice around the *Old Steine* at *Brighton*, from a Starting-place in the vicinity of the royal Pavilion in that Town.

A Day & an Hour being allotted for the Attempt, feveral Ladies attended to witnefs the diminutive Sir John take on the Burden of the fizeable Lord Cholmondeley. When all were affembl'd, Sir John defir'd His Lordfhip to diveft himfelf of all his Cloaths, to which Requeft the latter reply'd, *Strip ? Why, furely you promif'd to carry me in my Cloaths ?* Sir John was adamant, however, & anfwer'd, *By no means ! I engag'd to carry you, but not an Inch of Cloaths. Therefore, My Lord, make ready, & let us not difappoint the Ladies.* Lord Cholmondeley refuf'd vehemently to exhibit his Bulk in *puris naturalibus*, & Sir John was declar'd the Winner of the Wager by default.

R umours perfift moft ftubbornly that Sir John's Wife, Lady LETITIA LADE, is the former Inamorata of the executed High-Tobyman, *Sixteen-String* Jack.

OF MR. PITT's POWDER TAX, & ITS EFFECTS UPON FASHIONS IN HAIR, LED BY THE DUKE OF BEDFORD.

TO the confternation of the Whiggifh Nobility, the Prime Minifter, Mr. WILLIAM PITT, inftigated his POWDER TAX on the 5th of *May* this year, whereby any perfon wifhing to ufe hair-powder is obliged to vifit a Stamp Office, enter their name in a ledger, and purchafe a certificate permitting them to buy the faid powder at a tax of 1 Guinea per annum. Yet if Mr. Pitt hopes that this curious expedient will affift in paying for our war againft *France*, he might find himfelf gravely difappointed.

H is Grace the DUKE of BEDFORD feeks to confound the Prime Minifter by leaving off the ufe of powder entirely, and efchews tied hair in favour of a fingularly fhort ftile, which is become known as the *Bedford Crop.* We hear that he has contracted wagers with his friends to follow his example, and they appear happy to do fo.

T he late poor harvefts having engendered much difcontent, an attack was made upon the KING on the 29th of *October* by a hungry mob – who fmafhed the window of his coach as he proceeded to *Parliament,* and chanted NO WAR ! NO FAMINE ! NO GEORGE ! DOWN WITH PITT ! and GIVE US BREAD ! – and afforded the Prime Minifter a pretext upon which to put forward his Treafon and Sedition Bills.

On the 16th of this month, Mr. CHARLES JAMES FOX attended a publick meeting, at which he gave an oration on the fubject of Mr. Pitt's Bills. Mr. Fox's hair was cropped very clofe, and he wore no trace of powder. We underftand that the DUKE of BRADFORD was alfo in attendance, and did likewife.

AN ACCOUNT OF THE DUEL FOUGHT BY LORD VALENTIA & MR. HENRY GAWLER IN HAMBURG.

OUR War with *France* obliges honourable Gentlemen feeking to fettle their differences with Piftols or Blades to journey to other Nations if they wifh to evade judicial Confequences in *England.*

A Difpute having broke out between Lord VALENTIA & Mr. HENRY GAWLER, concerning the Criminal Converfation of the latter's elder Brother with the former's Wife, thefe Two Gentlemen took their Quarrel & their Firearms to *Hamburg,* in the company of their refpective Seconds & Surgeons. On the 28th of laft Month, Mr. Gawler's Hat was perforated by a fhot from Lord Valentia, who was likewife hit in the Breaft-bone by his Antagonift's ball, tho' his Surgeon was able to remove it at the fcene.

Lord Valentia fecur'd £200 in his Crim. Con. cafe againft Mr. JOHN GAWLER. His Lordfhip's Wife, Lady ANNE, is the Sifter of Vifcount WILLIAM Kitty COURTENAY, who was embroil'd in fodomitickal Intrigue, with Mr. WILLIAM BECKFORD, when he was but Ten Years of Age. Lady Anne has borne Two Children, one of whom her Hufband cannot with any certainty call his own, & another who is affuredly the baftard Progeny of the virile Mr. Gawler.

RUSPINI's BALSAMIC STYPTIC, for internal and external Bleedings, Wounds, &c.

Hereunder is the Size of the Ball that of late paffed through a Man's Cheek, dividing the *Vena Jugularis* on both fides, which bleeding was immediately ftopped by the Styptic, when no other means could give relief.

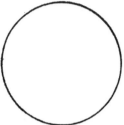

In confequence of this furprifing effect of the Styptic, Sir JOHN BORLASE WARREN has liberally ordered a quantity to be furnifhed to each Veffel of his Squadron, for the ufe of the Seamen, in difficult cafes.

The Styptic is to be had wholefale and retail of the CHEVALIER RUSPINI, *Pall-Mall* ; SURGEON-DENTIST to His Royal Highnefs The PRINCE of WALES ; & alfo his DENTIFRICE POWDER & TINCTURE, for the Preferving & Beautifying of the Teeth & Gums, & his ELIXIR for the Cure of the Tooth-ache.

BILIOUS OBSTRUCTION, GOUT, JAUNDICE, ASTHMATIC GOUT, & CHOLIC. Dr. BLENKENSOP's BILIOUS SPECIFIC ; Or, UNIVERSAL PREVENTIVE PILLS

Prepared by Mr. TAPLIN, Medical Difpenfary, *Edgeware-road, London.*

FOR coftive habits of every defcription, age, & conftitution ; they expeditioufly & almoft imperceptibly remove obftinate obftructions in the ftomach or inteftinal canal ; in early attacks of the gout they nearly amount to a fpecific ; in fevere & obftinate coughs they afford immediate relief, by reducing the contents of the ftomach, & leffening the preffure upon the lobes of the lungs ; in fhort, families having thefe pills in ufe will feldom find occafion for further medical affiftance.

BEFORE   AFTER

OF THE INIQUITOUS SALE OF A WIFE.

ON Friday laſt, a Butcher put a Halter about his Wife's Neck, & another about her Waiſt, & took her to the *Ram Inn,* at *Smithfield Market,* where ſhe was tied to a Railing, & offer'd for ſale. The Butcher ſecur'd 3 Guineas & a Crown from the happy Purchaſer, a Hog-driver.

This method amongſt the Lower Orders of diſſolving a Marriage is often employ'd by a Huſband & Wife when they have grown irredeemably weary of each other, & have agreed to go their ſeparate ways. The Wife is auction'd to the higheſt Bidder at a Market, as if ſhe were a Milch-cow or a Brood-mare. The Purchaſer is generally ſettl'd upon before ſuch a Sale, ſince it can ſcarcely be credited that a Female would acquieſce to this Indignity without the certain Knowledge that a Purchaſer will be found.

PARTICULARS CONCERNING THE BOOKSELLER, MR. JAMES LACKINGTON, & HIS MUCH ADMIR'D TEMPLE OF THE MUSES.

THERE cannot be any perſon in *London* who is not aware of one its foremoſt modern Wonders, Mr. LACKINGTON's *Temple of the Muſes,* but our provincial readers will perhaps enjoy a brief deſcription of it.

The Temple is located at No. 32, *Finſbury-place South,* has a frontage 140 Ft. in length, and the legend *The Cheapeſt Bookſeller in the World* is emblazoned over its door. Atop the building is a dome, upon which flies a flag, but only when Mr. Lackington is in reſidence. There is a wide ſair-caſe, which leads to lounging-rooms and expanſive book-caſes, the numberleſs contents of which Mr. Lackington buys in huge quantities at the loweſt rates, and ſells to his patrons at the moſt inexpenſive prices, the books within the Temple becoming ever cheaper as one aſcends through the galleries. Located centrally within the commodious premiſes is a circular counter ſo large that a Coach-and-ſix was driven around it, ſhortly after the eſtabliſhment firſt opened for trading.

Anything on Horſe-breeding?

Third Floor, Sir.

LATELY PUBLISHED:

A NEW & COMPLETE COLLECTION OF TRIALS for ADULTERY: Or A GENERAL HISTORY of MODERN GALLANTRY & DIVORCES.

Containing

All the moſt remarkable TRIALS heard & determined in the Courts of Doctors – Commons, the King's Bench, &c, &c. for ADULTERY, FORNICATION, CRUELTY, INCEST, & other CRIMINAL CONVERSATION, IMPOTENCY, &c. from the Year 1780 to the Middle of the Year 1797 ; including genuine Narratives of ILLEGAL ELOPEMENTS, UNEQUAL MARRIAGES, CALEDONIAN EXCURSIONS, PRIVATE INTRIGUES, ILLICIT AMOURS, &c. of many Characters in the moſt elevated Spheres of Life ; every Scene & Tranſaction, however ridiculous, whimſical, or extraordinary, is fairly repreſented, as becomes a faithful Hiſtorian ; the Whole taken in Short-hand by a Civilian of DOCTORS' COMMONS. Embelliſhed with an ELEGANT SET of PLATES, repreſenting the moſt ſtriking Scenes deſcribed in the Work.

Printed for the Proprietors by J. GILL ; Sold at the Shops of PARSONS & HOGG, in *Paternoſter-Row* : & may be had of all the Bookſellers, Newſcarriers, &c. in every Part of *Great Britain* & *Ireland.*

The Gin-Lane Gazette

PUBLISHED in LONDON   *June, 1798.*   Nathaniel Crowquill Efq.

AN ACCOUNT OF THE DUEL FOUGHT BY THE FIRST LORD OF THE TREASURY, MR. WILLIAM PITT, & MR. GEORGE TIERNEY M.P.

THREE O'Clock in the Afternoon, 27th of MAY - A Quarrel having erupted in the *Houfe of Commons* between the Prime Minifter, Mr. WILLIAM PITT, & the Member for *Southwark,* the *Whig* Mr. GEORGE TIERNEY, Honour was fatisfy'd with Piftols in the Vicinity of the Gibbet on *Putney-heath.* Both Parties afterwards quit the Duelling-ground uninjur'd.

Laft Month, Mr. Pitt had fought to fhepherd through the Houfe certain Amendments to the Legiflation governing the Procurement of Naval Recruits, the manning of His Majefty's Service being an urgent confideration at this time of War. Mr. Tierney raif'd Objections to the Propofals of Mr. Pitt, who accuf'd his Antagonift of harbouring a defire to obftruct the defence of the Country, & call'd into queftion the integrity of Mr. Tierney's Patriotifm. Mr Tierney's Demand that Mr. Pitt retract his Calumnies was rebuff'd, & a Challenge was iffu'd the Day following, which the Prime Minifter readily accepted.

The Speaker of the Houfe, Mr. HENRY ADDINGTON, attended as a Witnefs, & the difputatious Gentlemen ftood Twelve paces apart, each brandifhing a Brace of Piftols. All Four Shots fail'd to meet their Targets, & we believe Mr. Pitt fir'd his Second Ball harmlefsly into the air - an Expedient which the Ladies might care to know is call'd *delopement* by the duelling Fraternity.

This Prime Minifterial Duel has become a Well-fpring of vociferous Debate & Condemnation, & the greater part of publick Difapprobation is directed towards Mr. Pitt for putting himfelf in Harm's way at this time of national Peril. Mr. Addington is likewife cenfur'd for permitting the Altercation to burgeon so egregioufly, & Mr. WILLIAM WILBERFORCE has given Notice of his Intention to put forward a Motion againft the Principle of Duels.

His Majefty the KING wrote to Mr. Pitt on the 30th of laft Month, & exprefs'd a Wifh never to fee a Repetition of what had happen'd. He conceded that it perhaps could not have been avoided, but infifted that publick Characters have no right to weigh alone what they owe to themfelves, & that they fhould confider alfo what is due to their Country.

Price: Sixpence

PARTICULARS CONCERNING CAPT. CHARLES MORRIS'S RIBALD BALLAD ON THE ALGERIAN AMBASSADOR'S PRODIGIOUSLY-PROPORTION'D PIZZLE.

WE are much troubl'd by the Intelligence that Capt. CHARLES MORRIS's entertaining Ditty, *The Plenipotentiary* – which concerns itfelf with the coloffal Dimenfions of a foreign Dignitary's privy parts – will lead to Profecutions for Obfcenity. It is not for frolickfome or falacious Purpofes that we choofe to publifh here fundry lines from the work, therefore, but in order to fhew Solidarity with thofe Printers who have done nothing worfe than enjoy an *Englifhman's* right to Freedom of Speech, Word, & Thought.

THE Song begins with a fhort Defcription of the Gentleman felected by the Dey of Algiers for the Tafk of attending upon the *Englifh* Court :

> He fearched the Divan, till he found out a man,
> Whofe Bollocks were heavy and hairy,
> And he lately came o'er, from the Barbary fhore,
> As the great Plenipotentiary.
> When to *England* he came, with his pr——k in a flame,
> He fhewed it his Hoftefs on landing,
> Who fpread its renown thro' all parts of the Town,
> As a Pintle paft all underftanding.

The Ladies of the Town refolve to examine in perfon the Gentleman's celebrated Organ of Generation, & to venture beyond the Pleafure of a fimple ocular Infpection :

> The Dames of Intrigue formed their c——ts in a league
> To take him in turn like good folk, Sirs,
> The young Miffes' plan was to catch as catch can,
> And all were refolved on a ftroke, Sirs !

The Plenipotentiary foon has the good Fortune to fample the Charms of many eager Ladies of our Shores, who take it in turn to favour his fingular Phyfickal attribute :

> The next to be tried was an Alderman's bride,
> With a c——t that could fwallow a Turtle,
> Who had horned the dull brows of her worfhipful Spoufe,
> Till they fprouted like Venus's myrtle.
> Through thick and through thin, bowel-deep he dafhed in,
> Till her q——m frothed like cream in a dairy,
> And expreffed by loud Farts fhe was ftrained in all parts
> By the Great Plenipotentiary.

After fundry lewd Epifodes of this nature, during which the whole Nation fell fick for the Tripoli pr——k, the Ballad concludes with a fond Tribute to the lucky Fellow & his enviable Member :

> Of love's fweet Reward meafured out by the Yard,
> The Turk's was moft bleft of Mankind, Sir,
> For his powerful Dart went home to the Heart
> Whether ftuck in before or behind, Sir.
> But no pencil can draw this long-donged Pawfhaw,
> Than each c——t-loving contemporary.
> But as pr——ks of the Game let's drink Health to the name
> Of the Great Plenipotentiary !

The Song brings Capt. Morris great Succefs & Acclaim, & he is afforded an Annuity of £200 by the PRINCE of WALES. He was elected to the Sublime Society of Beeffteaks in the Year 1785, & his Works are fung often by the DUKE of NORFOLK, Mr. CHARLES JAMES FOX, & others, at the convivial gatherings of that gaftronomickal Club.

OF THE EXECUTION OF COMMODORE CARACCIOLO,
SANCTION'D BY REAR-ADMIRAL NELSON, & HIS SUPPOS'D RESURRECTION.

27th of JUNE - THE Traitor, Commodore FRANCESCO CARACCIOLO, was try'd aboard HMS *Foudroyant*, anchor'd in the *Bay of Naples*. He was found Guilty of a charge of betraying his Sovereign, the KING of NAPLES, & of firing upon *La Minerva*, his former Flag-fhip, & the Order for his Execution to be carry'd out aboard that Veffel was fign'd by Rear-Admiral HORATIO NELSON. The Commodore's Body was thrown into the Sea after he was hang'd from the Yardarm.

I fee no Stiffs...

Some Days later, His Majefty KING FERDINAND was aboard Foudroyant, & was fhock'd by the grifly Sight of a refurrected Caracciolo, making his way towards the Ship upon the Waves, & in an upright Pofture. Sir WILLIAM HAMILTON, who was alfo aboard, attempted to affuage the King's Difcomfiture by quipping that it feem'd the late Commodore could not reft until he had crav'd a royal Pardon. It was later difcover'd that fome Friends of Caracciolo had recover'd his Corpfe, & employ'd Planks, Corks, & Weights in achieving this morbid & frightful Effect. Rear-Admiral Nelfon order'd the Body to be tow'd to *Santa Lucia*, & it was interr'd at the Fifhermen's Church of *Santa Maria La Catena*.

Caracciolo was a Prince of Greek Extraction, who learnt his Seamanfhip at the feet of our own late Admiral RODNEY. He deferted his King for the rebellious *Jacobin* Caufe in May of this Year, & after unfuccefsful naval Actions, was found hiding in a Well upon his Uncle's Eftate.

PARTICULARS CONCERNING
MR. HUMPHRY DAVY'S HAPPY EXPERIMENTS WITH LAUGHING-GAS.

This wondrous Gas will have ferious Applications, Sir!

Aye, Sir! Moft ferious!

AT Dr. THOMAS BEDDOES's PNEUMATICK INSTITUTION, at *Hotwells, Dowry-square*, in the City of *Briftol*, Mr. HUMPHRY DAVY has undertaken Experiments with the Gas Nitrous-oxide, which produces the moft remarkable Effects upon its Subjects, as a Confequence of which it has become known as Laughing-gas.

Dr. Beddoes is of the Opinion that the Inhalation of certain kinds of Gafes might prove ufeful in the Treatment of Confumption, which he eftimates carries away One in Four Britons, but Mr. Davy's Inveftigations have led him to entirely new realms of Poffibility. He has taken Nitrous-oxide upon feveral Occafions, & has recorded its thrilling & highly pleafurable Effects upon the Body & Mind. He has been known to cry out & fkip about the Room when under its influence, & afferts that it will moft affuredly offer new underftanding of the Secrets & Workings of the Mind.

The *Pneumatick Inftitution* is lately become a fafhionable Eftablifhment, to the Salons of which flock Poets, Natural Philofophers, Playwrights, Surgeons, & fundry other Characters of Publick Life, & by means of this wondrous Gas they hope to give their Wits free rein to enjoy the moft elevated Spheres of Human Thought & Fancy. The Poet & Friend of Mr. Davy, Mr. ROBERT SOUTHEY, has partaken of it, & has faid that he feels fure the Air in Heaven muft be compof'd of this delightful Gas. Mr. SAMUEL TAYLOR COLERIDGE has likewife made Experiments with it, & claims to have attain'd a State of unmingl'd Pleafure, greater than anything he has heretofore achiev'd.

The SEVEN DIALS STROLLER

Of the lecherous OLD Q, & his MILK BATHS.

THE DUKE of QUEENSBURY has of late taken up a moſt novel Method of maintaining what little of his Youth and Vigour endures. Not content with applying to his ſunken Cheeks a brace of Veal-chops – which he afterwards gives to his Dogs – he now takes Baths of Milk, in the hope that theſe Expedients will rejuvenate his wizen'd old Carcaſs.

The Duke performs theſe Ablutions in warm Milk, perfum'd with powder of Almonds, at Seven O'Clock each Morning, and takes Coffee and butter'd Muffins as he bathes. Thereafter, he retires to his Bed for a nap. Many Citizens of London have given up Milk for fear of drinking that which the Duke has uſ'd, as it is generally thought that he ſells it back to his Supplier when he is done with it.

I hate Milk when it gets a ſkin on it...

The Duke has long been known as *Old Q,* owing to that Letter being emblazon'd upon the Door of his Carriage. He has ever been a libidinous, rakiſh Goat, but his Potency ſeems to have abandon'd him in recent Years, as the following Intelligence will teſtify. He is lately reduc'd to engaging the ſervices of a Procureſs, who ſearches the Taverns, Boarding-ſchools, & Lodging-houſes for comely Wenches to ſatisfy his baſe Urges. Likely Females are brought to the Duke's Houſe at *Piccadilly,* & with a pipe of Tobacco clamp'd between his yellowing Teeth, he appraiſes them from behind a Screen. When he has choſen one who pleaſes his Fancy, he offers them the pretty ſum of Ten Guineas to diſrobe for his Gratification, yet he never lays a Finger upon them, his ability to crown his Luſt with phyſickal Poſſeſſion doubtleſs having fled many Years hence.

LOST

ON Wedneſday night the 5th of November, 1800, at Whitchurch, Hants.

A YOUNG POINTER DOG, with yellow ſpots ; anſwers to the name of BOUNCE.

Whoever will bring him to Mr. JOHN GODDEN, at *Hurſtbourne Park,* ſhall receive One Guinea reward.

N.B. Whoever detains him after this advertiſement ſhall ſuffer according to the law.

A YOUNG LADY, of reſpectability and character, amiable diſpoſition, property of Six Hundred Pounds, wiſhes to enter into the Married State, as ſhe is left without friends. Would give the preference to a military man, therefore none but an Adjutant or Quarter-Maſter of reſpectability need apply.

If any Gentleman wiſhes for farther particulars, by giving his reference, and writing to the Lady A.B. (poſt paid) at No. 452, *Strand, London,* he will receive information.

OF HER MAJESTY THE QUEEN'S CURIOUS CHRISTMAS-TREE.

HER MAJESTY Queen CHARLOTTE is importing a fingular cuftom from her native Duchy of *Mecklenburg-Strelitz.*

She has procured a large tub, and intends to plant in it a great Yew-tree, which fhe fhall exhibit indoors. This curious plan fhall be carried out on Chriftmas Day, at Queen's Lodge, *Windfor.* In an attempt to delight and amufe the children of the town's principal families, fhe will bedeck her Chriftmas-tree with candles, almonds, fruits, and trifling gifts of play-things.

Your perplexed correfpondent can only furmife that the royal offfpring will fear that, like His Majefty the KING, their mother has run irrevocably mad.

AN ACCOUNT OF HOW THE PRINCE OF WALES WAS ASTOUNDED BY HIS ROYAL BROTHER'S TREMENDOUS MEMBRUM VIRILE.

HIS Royal Highnefs the PRINCE of WALES lately delights in relating to any of his Circle who will liften how he firft became cognizant of the ample Proportions of the Penis with which one of his Siblings is blefs'd.

He was once travelling with his royal Brother in a Carriage, when the unnam'd PRINCE was compell'd to anfwer the call of Nature. After loofening his Breeches, he directed his mighty Pizzle out of the Window, & the Pifs flow'd out of him as Water does from a Fountain. The Driver thought that they had been overtaken by a Rain-ftorm, fo thunderous was the Cafcade from the Hanoverian Member, and he urg'd the Horfes onwards to efcape a Drenching.

Should we difcover which of the royal Brothers is fo happily endow'd, we fhall be glad to fhare the Intelligence with the Ladies.

MATRIMONY.

A GENTLEMAN under 40 years of age, moft refpectably fituated, refident in London, with found conftitution & excellent health, in face & perfon what is generally called a good-looking fellow, a chearful difpofition & good temper, in eafy circumftances as to fortune, and owes no man a fhilling, would be happy to meet a Lady about his own age, good tempered, in fimilar circumftances, and difpofed to Matrimony.——— Any Lady whom the above might fuit, by an intimation through the channel of this paper, addrefsed to G.L. will be attended on in perfon ; but not through a reprefentative. The truth & accuracy of the above defcription can, if required, be immediately realifed in the moft fatisfactory manner, & the ftricteft honour, & moft inviolable fecrecy may be fecurely depended upon.

EPILOGUE.

At this pass, worthier pens than mine would offer apposite & penetrating Observations upon the business of Editorship. It might be posited withal that a Half-century engag'd in the chronickling of the World's Triumphs, Trials & Tribulations should yield an abundance of Insights into the nature of Mankind. Yet I feel I can assist little on that head, & I am surely no Encomiast for my chosen Trade. Put plainly, 'tis nothing more than a business which keeps frail Body & weary'd Soul conjoin'd, & allows a fellow the Honour, on occasion, of spectating upon the deeds of Great Men. I shall confine myself, therefore, to a few brief remarks upon the Denouement of my dealings with The GIN-LANE GAZETTE.

Mr. STROAKER has prov'd himself a worthy Inheritor of the Crown of Editorship, & I am content to allow him to steer my *Gazette* upon a course of his own chusing. The continuing Wars with France, & the eccentricities of People of the First Distinction, may be rely'd upon to supply him with ample matter for our Readership, & the ensuing monetary Rewards should offer me a comforting Annuity in my Dotage. Even now, as I write, my Parlour is clutter'd with trunks & locking-boxes replete with my moveables, which I am shortly to have convey'd to my dear Sister's home. Rural domesticity proves most alluring after so many Years of metropolitan Clamour. I think it unlikely that bucolic Quietude shall inspire me to busy my Days with penning Novels, verses, or *Libretti* for comick Operas – diversions which many of my peers are inclin'd to take up with encroaching senility – for tho' the World is oft-times venal, capricious & exasperating, it has done nothing to merit such a Portion !

As for Mr. JAKES, I regret to report that his Fate is a most perplexing one. Within a Week of my making known the plan for my Decampment, he disappear'd, & has not been heard of since. Rumours abound that he found himself inundated to the very haunches in Debt to the Bully of a singularly iniquitous Bawdy-house, & betook himself to his Heels for fear of rough Treatment. I should be troubl'd but not in the least surpris'd if this were the Case. A scrofulous Dog he may be, but we weather'd many Storms together & in faith I wish him well.

'Tis time to leave off, & conscious though I am of my own Imperfections in the assembling of these sheets, I deliver them up humbly to publick Curiosity with assurances that

I remain

Your Friend & Servant to command,

Nathaniel Crowquill Esq.

FINIS.

LEXICON
Of WORDS & PHRASES ;

For the Benefit of PROVINCIALS
& BUMPKINS.

ABBESS : The Bawd, or Keeper, of a Brothel, known as a *Nunnery.*

AMOROUS FAIRS : Harlots & Whores.

BAGNIO : A Bath-houfe, where trade with Whores might alfo be procur'd.

BEAU MONDE : The fafhionable World, & thofe who are Members of it.

BILLS of MORTALITY : The Lifts iffu'd weekly, giving Particulars of the Numbers of Deceaf'd in *London*, & the Caufes of their deaths.

BLACKAMOOR : A *Negro,* or Perfon of *Africkan* origins.

BOMBAZEEN : Heavy cloth of Worfted, oft uf'd for Mourning-cloaths.

BON TON : Fafhionable & genteel Perfons of the Firft Rank.

BREECHES PLAYER : A Female Player, taking the part of a Man upon the Stage, & oft titillating her Audience in fo doing.

BULLY : A common Proftitute's Protector.

BUNG MY EYE : To drink a Draught, or Dram.

CALEDONIAN EXCURSIONS : Elopements to *Gretna Green,* for the purpofes of entering into Wedlock without parental Interceffion.

CHIRURGICKAL : Of the bufinefs of a Chirurgeon, or Surgeon.

CLOSE-STOOL : A Convenience, with a Receptacle for Night-foil.

CORNUTED : Having one's Head horn'd, in the manner of a Cuckold ; fuffering the Indignity of an unfaithful Wife.

CRIMINAL CONVERSATION [*oft abbreviated* to CRIM. CON.] : An Action of Common Law, whereby a Hufband feeks pecuniary Redrefs from a Third Party enjoying adulterous Dealings with his Wife.

CYPRIAN : A libidinous Perfon, in the manner of a Votary of the *Cyprian* goddefs, *Aphrodite.*

DOCTORS' COMMONS : The confiftory & ecclefiaftickal Court of *London,* with Powers of diffolving the religious Element of a Marriage.

EAU de LUCE : Smelling-falts.

FALLEN SISTERHOOD : The Whores of the Town.

THE FANCY : Thofe who follow the Prize-fight, & its Practitioners.

GALLANTRY : Amorous Intriguing with the fairer Sex.

GASCONADE : Boasting & Bluster.

HEADS : That part of a Ship where one answers the call of Nature.

HIGH-TOBYMAN : A mounted Gentleman of the *Toby*, or High-road ; a Highwayman.

MACARONI : A Gentleman of Fashion, who arrays himself in effeminate & gaudy Cloaths,
in the *French* or *Italian* stiles.

MOLLY-HOUSE : A House of Ill-fame, solely for, & frequented by, Sodomites.

NUNNERY : A Bawdy-house or Brothel, oft in the purlieus of *Covent-garden.*

OTAHEITE : An Island of the *South-Seas,* its name lately contracted to Tahiti.

PAWSHAW : A *Turk* of high Rank.

PERRUQUE : A Wig.

PINTLE : A Pin, or Bolt ; oft us'd to signify the Penis.

POSTURE MOLL : A female Hireling, oft in a state of undress, who adopts Attitudes
& Postures for the titillation of male Spectators.

PRIVITIES : The privy parts ; the Organs of Generation.

PURL : A Beverage made from Ale mull'd with Spices, lac'd with Gin, & oft mixt with sweeten'd Milk.

ROOKERIES : Dilapidated, disreputable, & crowded parts of the Town, where Delinquency & Malfeasance are rife.

SAL VOLATILE : Smelling-salts.

SANS-CULOTTES : Ragged-ars'd Revolutionaries of *France.*

SIXPENNY CUTS : Engravings sold at the Print-shops.

SPUNGING-HOUSE : A Gaol for the Detention of those who have yet to secure Bail.

STOCKJOBBERS : Those who trade in Stocks in the financial Houses of the City.

THREEPENNY-UPRIGHT : The Act of enjoying coital union while upon one's Feet,
with the meanest sort of common Prostitute ; that
which is also known as a *Knee-trembler* ; also the
Name for a Harlot who offers her Patrons this Service.

BIBLIOGRAPHY

The following volumes have proved invaluable in the aſſembling of theſe ſheets, and I am pleaſed to beſtow an honourable mention upon the online Oxford Dictionary of National Biography.

Bills, M. (2006) *The Art of Satire: London in Caricature,* London: Philip Wilſon Publiſhers.

Byrne, P. (2004) *Perdita: The Life of Mary Robinſon,* London: HarperCollins.

Chambers, P. (2006) *The Cock Lane Ghoſt: Murder, Sex and Haunting in Dr Johnson's London,* Stroud: Sutton Publiſhing Limited.

Christian, G. (1999) *Fragile Paradiſe,* Milſons Point: Doubleday.

Clayton, T. (2008) *Tars: The Men Who Made Britain Rule the Waves,* London: Hodder & Stoughton.

Clee, N. (2010) *Eclipſe: The Story of the Rogue, the Madam and the Horſe that Changed Racing,* London: Tranſworld Publiſhers.

Cruickſhank, D. (2009) *The Secret Hiſtory of Georgian London: How the Wages of Sin Shaped the Capital,* London: Random Houſe Books.

Dening, G. (1992) *Mr Bligh's Bad Language: Paſſion, Power and Theatre on the Bounty,* New York: Univerſity of Cambridge.

Foreman, A. (1999) *Georgiana Ducheſs of Devonſhire,* London: HarperCollins.

Gatrell, V. (2006) *City of Laughter: Sex and Satire in Eighteenth-Century London,* London: Atlantic Books.

Hibbert, C. (1998) *George III: A Perſonal Hiſtory,* London: Viking.

Hibbert, C. (2004) *King Mob,* Stroud: Sutton Publiſhing Limited.

Hickman, K. (2003) *Courteſans,* London: Harper Perennial.

Hopton, R. (2007) *Piſtols at Dawn: A Hiſtory of Duelling,* London: Portrait.

Lonſdale, R. (ed.) (1987) *The New Oxford Book of Eighteenth Century Verſe,* Oxford: Oxford Univerſity Preſs.

Lord, E. (2010) *The Hell-Fire Clubs: Sex, Sataniſm and Secret Societies,* Connecticut: Yale Univerſity Preſs.

Lowry, J. (2006) *Fiddlers and Whores: The Candid Memoirs of a Surgeon in Nelſon's Fleet,* London: Chatham Publiſhing.

Manning, J. (2005) *My Lady Scandalous: The Amazing Life and Outrageous Times of Grace Dalrymple Elliott, Royal Courteſan,* New York: Simon & Schuſter.

Mitchell, L.G. (1997) *Charles James Fox,* London: Penguin.

Nokes, D. (2010) *Samuel Johnſon: A Life,* London: Faber and Faber.

O'Connell, S. (2003) *London 1753,* London: The Britiſh Muſeum Preſs.

Porter, R. (2003) *Quacks: Fakers and Charlatans in Medicine,* Stroud: Tempus Publiſhing Limited.

Rubenhold, H. (2005) *Harris's Liſt of Covent-Garden Ladies: Sex in the City in Georgian Britain,* Stroud: Tempus Publiſhing Limited.

Stark, S.J. (1998) *Female Tars: Women Aboard Ship,* London: Pimlico.

Stone, L. (1992) *Road to Divorce: England 1530–1987,* Oxford: Oxford Univerſity Preſs.

Tillyard, S. (2007) *A Royal Affair: George III and his Troubleſome Siblings,* London: Vintage.

Uglow, J. (2003) *The Lunar Men: The Friends Who Made the Future,* London: Faber and Faber.

White, T.H. (2000) *The Age of Scandal,* London: Penguin.

SUBSCRIBERS

Unbound is a new kind of publiſhing houſe. Our books are funded directly by readers. This was a very popular idea during the late eighteenth and early nineteenth century. Now we have revived it for the internet age. It allows authors to write the books they really want to write and readers to ſupport the writing they would moſt like to ſee publiſhed.

The names liſted below are of readers who have pledged their ſupport and made this book happen. If you'd like to join them, viſit: www.unbound.co.uk.

Foundation Patron
This book was made poſſible by a very generous foundation pledge from the ThoughtOut Project at UEA

Thomas Abert	Kat Brown	Jennifer Dellow	Liſa Gee
Geoff Adams	Tim Bryars	Elaine Deniſon	Tina Louiſe Gibbons
Paul Adamſon	Victoria Buckley	JF Derry	Simon Gibſon
Chris Addiſon	Jonathan Bullock	John Dexter	Davina Gifford
Wyndham Albery	Corrinne Burns	Emma Dickens	Peter Gill
Katie Allinſon	Marcus Butcher	Natalie Dorey	David Gilray
Michael Angus	Caroline Butler	Judith Downey	Suzanne Gotro
Judy Anthony	Ian Buxton	Ruth Downie	Annie Gray
Helen Armfield	Stephanie C	Keith Dunbar	Muriel Gray
Lucy Armſtrong	Nick Cambridge	Beth Dunn	Katherine Green
Philippa Arthan	Xander Canſell	Vivienne Dunſtan	Andy Grigg
Avenue Books	Shereen Carroll	Terence Egalton	John Grindrod
Clare Axton	Caitlin Cartwright	Liſa Elliott	Dan Groenewald
Melanie Backe-Hanſen	Suſan Catto	Markman Ellis	Katrina Gulliver
Chris Baker	Jeanneane Ceſvette	Matthias Embid	Tim Guthat
Brian Balfour-Oatts	Elaine Chalus	Karen Evans	Liz Hanbury
Kriſta Ball	Claire Chambers	Sharon Eyre	Sue Hanley
Graham Barnetſon	Jonathan Cheetham	Peter Falconer	Eleanor Harris
Dana Barrett	Helen Cheſſhire	Falkland Arms	Irene Harris
Cat Barton	Glynn Chriſtian	Gregory Fenby Taylor	Caitlin Harvey
Arpinder Baryana	Valerie Chriſtie	Robert Ferguſon	Haven Riſk Management
Sophie Baſbayon	Allan Clark	Charles Fernyhough	Dave Hawkins
Karen Baſton	Andrew Clark	Abigail Fine	Claire Hayward
Matthew Bate	Melanie Clegg	Anne Fine	Sheila Heeps
Patrick Baty	Kenny Clements	Richard Fitch	Jude Henderſon
Richard Bennett	David Coke	Roger Fitzhugh	Mark Henderſon
Carole Benſon	Stevyn Colgan	Chriſſy Fleps	Bob Hendley
Rebecka Berg	Gina Collia-Suzuki	Evelyn Foley	Samuel Henley
Terry Bergin	Joy Conway	Nicholas Fooks	E O Higgins
Les Beſſant	Lewis Cook	Alan Ford	Jane Hill
Paul Birch	Eamonn Cooper	Charly Ford	Shelley Hill
Katarina Birkedal	Carol Cragoe	Julia Forte	Robert Hoare
Tony Boullemier	Steve Crummaford	Ilana Fox	Siobhan Hoffmann Heap
Chris Boulton	Heather Culpin	Jonathan Foyle	Stephen Hoppe
Victoria Bowers Coulſon	Silas Currie	Henry France	George Hornby
Michael Bowman	Babs Dada	Philippa Francis	Julian Humphrys
Chris Brace	Peter Dalling	Jens Franke	Henri Hunter
Peter Brace	Valerie Daly	Iſobel Frankiſh	Liſa Hunter
Catharine Braithwaite	Ian Daly-Smith	Liz Fraſer	Cathy Hurren
Emily Brand	Karen Darby	Emma Curtis & Andrew	Suſanne Huttner
Donal Brannigan	Louiſe Davies	Maginley, The Frolick	Majeed Jabbar
Lucinda Brant	Suſannah Davis	Robert Froſt-Stevenſon	Graham Jackſon
Anna Brickman	Belinda Daws	Ian Furbank	Leo James
Adam Brown	Phil Day	Jon Gardner	Greg Jenner
David Brown	Gina Decio	Steve Gardner	Helena Jenſen

David Johnson
Jacqueline Johnstone
Rhona Johnstone
Alan Jones
Amanda Jones
Emily Jones
Julie Jones
Lora Jones
Terry Jones
Peter Jukes
Robert Justice
Andrea Kamphuis
Patricia Keatung
Peter Kemp
Dan Kieran
Paul Kingett
Stewart Kirk
Fi Kirkpatrick
Narell Klingberg
Doreen Knight
India Knight
Graham Knowles
Laura Knox
Brian Lambie
John Lanigan
Adele Lawson
Paul Lay
Jude Leavy
Emery Lee
Richard Lee
Shani Lee
Anthony Lewis
Beth Lewis
Tiran Lewis
Pete Lindsay
Eva Lippold
Marguerite Lipscomb
Suzannah Lipscomb
David Lister
Sheila Littleton
Jacqui Livesey
Robert Llewellyn
Sue Llewellyn
George Lloyd
Robert Loch
Kari Long
Suzanne Louail
Katy Lowe
Kayla Lowes
Joanne Lucas
Rob Lucas
David Ludlow
Sophie McAllister
Amanda Jane McCartney
Matthew McCormack
Amanda McCormick

Kyle McCreary
Karen McDonnell
Mo McFarland
Louise Mackenzie
Fiona McNeil
Olivia McNulty
Kate Madigan
Philippa Manasseh
Chris Marrum
Sian Meadowcroft
Joel Meadows
Hilary Meehan
Anna Melville-James
Philip Metcalfe
Deborah Metters
Joel Mishon
John Mitchinson
Ronald Mitchinson
Fiona Mitford
James Moakes
Stephen Mold
Leonardo Monno
Michael Moran
Kate Morant
Paul Mortimer
Rachel Mosses
Rebecca Muecke
Jenni Murphy
James Naylor
Andrew Neve
Susan Newbould
Scott James William
  Newnham
David Newsome
Julie Niven
Vaun Earl Norman
Beverley North
Lauren O'Connell
Jim O'Donnell
Jenny O'Gorman
Ole Petter Olsen
Sally Osborn
Mark Ossowski
Asta Ottey
Damien Owens
Karen Page
Debbie Pakulski
Julia Parker
Kevin Parker
Mike Paterson
Caroline & James Pennock
Adam Pepper
Julie Philipson
Patricia Phillips
James Phillpotts
Catherine Phipps

William Pickwell
Justin Pollard
Geoff Pollock
Lin Pollock
Matthew Porter
Hazel Potter
Lee Price
Kitty Pridden
Christopher Pridham
Father Prout
Laura Purcell
Huan Quayle
Catherine Quinn
Maria Raich
Idham Ramadi
Caroline Rance
Katie Rawlins
Karen Redman
Mike Rendell
Jacqueline Riding
Wyn Roberts
Croash Robinson
Roberto Rosele
Kate Rosser Frost
Hallie Rubenhold
Susan Ruth
Gemma Rutterford
Marie Ryal
Juliet Salmon
Rebecca Sams
Gudrun Schwarz
Nicola Scull
Jaqueline Sellers
Dick Selwood
Jessica Sharkey
Catherine Shaw
Diane Shaw
Matt Shaw
Natalie Shaw
Steve Shorrock
Alexandra Sills
Cathy Simpson
Michael Smeeth
Linda Smith
Tim Smith
Adam Smithson
Mo Smyth
David Somers
Kirsty Staunton
Annie Stevens
Adam Stevenson
Jessica Stevenson
Victoria Stoett
Emma Stokes
Adam Stone
Peter Stone

Tom Sykes
Andrew Szkuta
Sandra Teal
Grace Tebbutt
Jayne Thomas
Bill Thompson
David Thornton
Jeremy Timms
Jackie Titmuss
Kim Tolley
Liz Townsend
Sarah Tregear
David Tubby
Andrew Turner
Simon & Pamela T-W
Sophia Ufton
Kristina VanHeefswijk
Mark Vent
David Waller
Heather Walsh
Sheila Mary Watt
Nerys Watts
Robert Webb
Heather Werrell
Jen Westcott
Maximillian Whiteford
Andrew Wiggins
Helen Williams
Ian Williams
Kate Williams
Mark J J Williams
Chris Wilton
Dianne Wilton
Stuart Witts
Will Wivell
Ian Wolf
Dar Wolnik
Debbie Wood
Rob Wood
Julian Woodford
Kirstin Woodward
Barbara Wright
Rachel Wright
Simon York
Jane Young
Jane Zara
Andrea Zuvich

A NOTE ON TYPE

There are a dozen or fo typefaces ufed in *The Gin-Lane Gazette,* moft of them modern copies of 18th-century fonts, many or them broken or 'dirty'. Perhaps the moft ftriking difference for modern readers is the ufe of the long 's' – printed 'f' in roman and '*ſ*' in italic. This letter was ufed at the beginning and in the middle of words, but not at the end, hence 'bufinefs', 'fong' and 'ufe'. There are other exceptions – the fhort 's' is ufed before or after the letter 'f', or before the letters 'b' and 'k', but the bafic rule – never at the end – is the moft important.

The long 's' is thought to have originated in the Ancient Greek diftinction between the normal letter *ſigma* (σ) and a fpecial form ufed at the end of words (ς). Becaufe fo many of the early typographers and printers from the Renaiffance onwards were familiar with Ancient Greek, this convention paffed over into other European languages including Englifh, where it remained prevalent until the end of the 18th century.

Gradually the confufion with the roman letter 'f' led typefetters to abandon it. Influential modern typefaces fuch as thofe defigned by Giambattifta Bodoni (1740–1813) and Pierre Didot (1760–1853) had no long 's' nor did William Bell's edition of Shakefpeare's works in 1788. His advertifement made the reafons clear:

'In the mode of printing too, he hath ventured to depart from the common mode, by rejecting the long ſ in favour of the round one, as being leſs liable to error from the occaſional imperfections of the letter f, and the frequent ſubſtitution of it for the long ſ.'

Finally, in 1803, the letter f received a blow from which it was never to recover: *The Times* changed to a modern typeface with no long 's'. The letter furvives only in books like this one, which feek to celebrate fome of the loft qualities of times paft.